COPYRIGHT

Published by:
SeeMore's Publishing House,
Noosa Heads, Queensland, Australia.
ISBN: 978-0-6451665-0-7

PUBLICATION INFORMATION

The information and stories provided in this book are based on the author's personal experiences of working with thousands of children in the health and education sectors for more than 40 years. In some cases, the names of the children in the stories have been changed to protect their privacy.

When bad things happen...

good things can grow

Survivors' stories of hope from the aftermath
of unimaginable trauma, abuse and burns.

DR SUSIE O'NEILL

When I was 5 years old,
my mother always told me
that happiness was the key to life.
When I went to school, they asked me
what I wanted to be when I grew up.
I wrote down 'happy'.
They told me I didn't understand the
assignment, and I told them they
didn't understand life.

- JOHN LENNON

Finding Purpose

Sometimes the bad things that happen in our lives put us directly on the path to the best things that will ever happen to us - Nicole Reed. Every life has a purpose.

The sliding doors of life really fascinates me. I have a "things happen for a reason," "it was meant to be," "out of bad things, good things happen" mentality. It actually drives my husband quite mad, and he oftens says, "How can you turn that one into a positive?" So, I guess I'm a "glass half full" sort of person. Being happy, doing things for others that make them happy, is what makes me happy. Over time, I have come to value three things that are most important to me in others - trust, loyalty, and kindness - and the thing that gets me through really challenging times, a bit of determination.

It is through the unimaginable tragedies of others I found my purpose. Guiding them to find strength through hope to be able to triumph over adversity and be happy. I would love to take ownership of all that they had accomplished, truth being they were responsible for what they had achieved all by themselves once they gained my trust. Working with hundreds of survivors of unbelievable trauma and pain I have learnt that from bad things, good things can grow and when you are given hope you can find happiness.

I realise how precious life is, probably because I've seen how it can be taken away.

- PIERCE BROSNAN

Sketch by artist Maryanne Lillecrapp - www.maryanne.com.au
2021

Some of us think holding on makes us strong but sometimes it is letting go...

- HERMANN HESSE

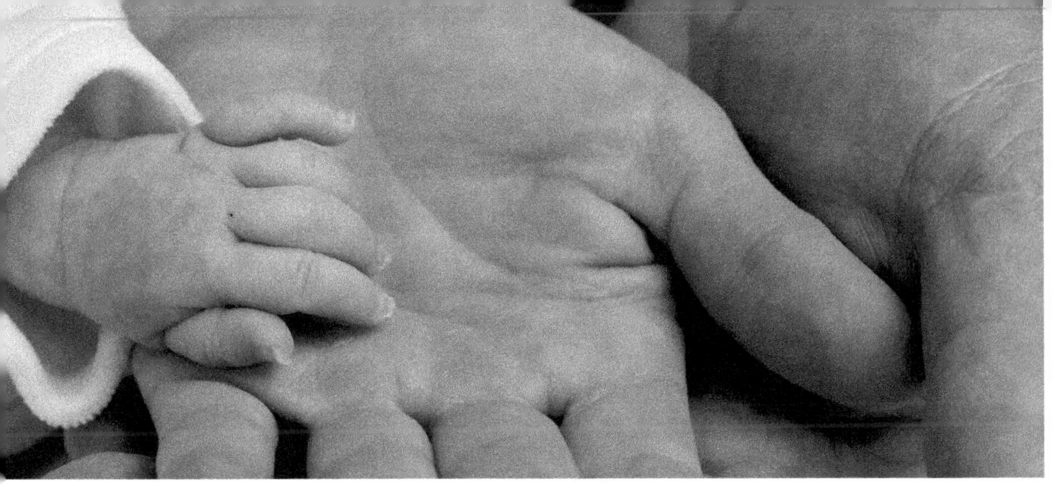

Bella

We got to hold her in our hands for a little while but will hold her in our hearts forever.

This is not how I had planned to dedicate this book, but this little person certainly has a beautiful story to tell and show how "When bad things happen, good things can grow".

Bella this book is dedicated to you.

It was in December on a family holiday that our daughter Emma shared the news with us that she was having a little girl. We were over the moon. That's not to say the six boys are any less loved, it was just that Nellie was surrounded by brothers and male cousins and was desperate to have a little sister in the family. When Lewi her younger brother arrived, she was in denial for quite a few weeks and renamed him Millie. But now she wouldn't change him for the world. With Nellie's excitement of having a sister, her dad Adam and Emma allowed her to choose the name. From that moment she was known as Bella, unbeknown to us, Bella meaning beautiful.

Then the news came that little Bella inside may have some challenges, it was the start of a six-month rollercoaster ride. The way Emma and Adam handled each misdiagnosis was admirable. Every time there was a sign of a health issue, Bella would prove them wrong. The conclusion was that she was a much smaller baby than her nine-pound siblings. By Christmas things were looking promising. The journey was something to remember, so for Emma and Adam's Christmas present, I wrote a song and had it recorded, called ''I Believe in Miracles, Bella the Miracle is You''.

Bella is certainly that, she is a miracle, she was not missing out on our world. She defied all odds to meet her family. Bella Margy Gwen arrived at 3:33 p.m. (3 our lucky number) on April 28, 2021, and it was such a relief when they announced she was perfect!

Then, 24 hours later our original fears began to become a reality. Bella's fight to live started all over again. The movement in her arms and legs were slowing and she needed help to breath. Bella was transferred to Monash Children's Hospital in Melbourne where we painstakingly watched her endure test after test. Every day we would wake up and walk into the hospital thinking they would say things have turned around, Bella is going to be okay. We were so full of hope, we could not have fathomed what was about to come next. At fifteen days old she was diagnosed with SMA (Spinal Muscular Atrophy) a degenerative condition. Bella was struggling, there was no treatment, no cure, and she would not survive. Not only was it a miracle that Bella had survived her birth, but a miracle they found a cause. She had been chosen for this family, she had something to tell us that would change our families for generations to come. Bella has given us a precious gift, "knowledge", knowledge that the genetic condition SMA exists in our families and can now be detected so that future babies and their families would not have to experience the heartbreaking pain we have.

Bella was known to the special care nurses as a little bright spark. They put pictures in her crib of animals and shapes to keep her occupied, when those big eyes were taking everything in. Sometimes she would lie awake for hours and look at you as if to say, "I know what is going on."

In a way, Bella has written her own life story and planned it right to the end. Emma and Adam went to the hospital knowing the inevitable. Bella peacefully passed away, so they thought. After several minutes, the doctors were called to pronounce her death, but Bella still had more to do, she hadn't had time to say goodbye to her big brothers and sister. So, to the medical fraternity surprise, those big eyes popped open with an "I'm back" look as her dad bent down to kiss her. We arrived at the hospital to see her wide awake and give her our last goodbye kisses. Minutes later at 11:11 a.m. on May 18, 2021, her beautiful soul left the room on her way to heaven, leaving us with her warm cuddly body to treasure for a few more hours.

Emma was under the guidance of a very experienced obstetrician. He, like other doctors we have spoken with since was unaware of SMA, even though SMA is the leading genetic disorder cause of death in children under the age of two in Australia. We have also recently learned 1 in 35 people are carriers of SMA and if both parents are carriers, as in Emma and Adams case, there is a 25% chance of having a child with SMA. A simple blood test exists that could have alerted to the fact that they were both carries. We want to make sure our pain and Bella's life has a purpose. There are things that can be done, prevention by offering a simple saliva test or blood test that is available now and educating doctors and obstetricians about these tests. Also offering screening through the heal prick test that is already done to all babies after birth. If SMA is diagnosed before degeneration occurs there are treatments available. The earlier this is detected the better chance a baby has of survival and/or a life without a disability. The only state and territory in Australia offering heal prick tests is NSW and ACT, and this is already saving babies lives.

We are so grateful to have had Bella in our lives. She touched our hearts in more ways than we could have ever imagined. Bella reminded us that health and family is what matters most. The love we experienced was deeper than we could have imagined, as was the pain we felt from a broken heart. We found a deeper family connection that has brought us even closer together. We are so proud of Emma, Adam, and the children and how they have coped with this heartbreaking journey. They have taught us that strength is not holding on, it is letting go. And I have learnt that heartache can be more painful than a physical wound. Bella, you are our real-life miracle angel.

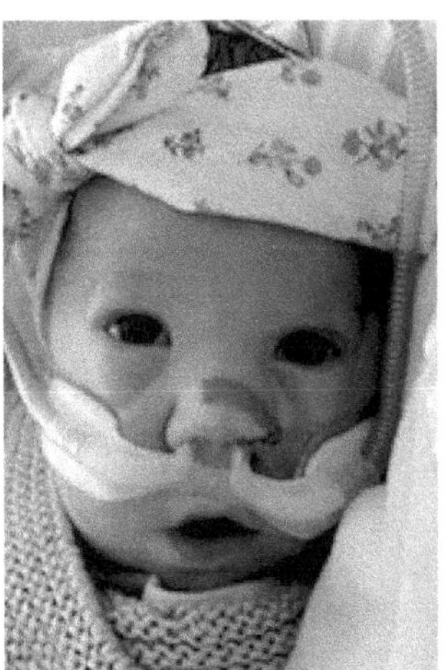

Contents

Susie with Brittney, Dalton and David

One child, one teacher,
one book, one pen
can change the world.

- MALALA YOUSAFZAI

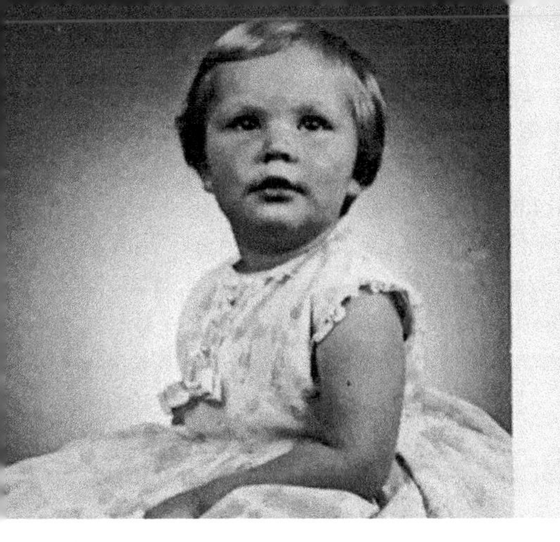 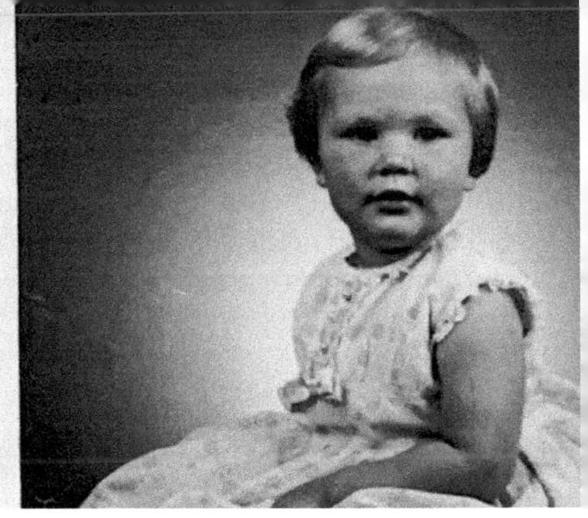

CHAPTER ONE

My Story

Everybody has a story, don't be too quick to judge

Dr. Susie O'Neill

My happiest memories growing up were picking blackberries and daffodils with my sister Mandy, brother Simon, and our cousins, and then trying to make our fortune by selling them in stalls we had set up on the side of the road, usually selling them to our aunts and uncles. Other favourites were Dad's make-believe stories that took us on amazing adventures or his adaption of folktales like the story of Rumpelstiltskin. It's the story of a miller who gets his daughter into a troubled situation by falsely telling the king she spins straw into gold, and Rumpelstiltskin gets her out of the situation in return for her possessions. The problem was I had inherited a vivid imagination and believed most of his stories. At the age of around four, my parents found me with a bike wheel, fruit box spinning-wheel contraption I had made, trying to spin straw into gold. Weekends often included spending time at my Nana's. Along with my mother, she is the person to this day I admire most. She was kind, non-judgemental, funny, and a great cook who even made livers taste nice. Nana would often have her 20 grandchildren stay at her home at one time. Nothing was ever too much trouble. She used to buy Christmas presents for everyone in the family - 33 of us plus extras, but would get them all mixed up. Sometimes you would end up with a pair of jocks or two left shoes. Opening the presents was the funniest time, and Nana would laugh just as hard.

My dad was a well-known potter (ceramic artist). So well known, in fact, I remember a road trip to Pro Hart's home in Broken Hill when we were very young, where my dad swapped two of his ceramic pots for two Pro Hart paintings. In 1968, Dad won a scholarship to rewrite the "Creative Activities Program" for Victorian Primary Schools. We were never allowed to have colouring books during our childhood as Dad believed it restricted our creative ability. We were given blank sheets of paper, pencils, and paint, and of course a slab of clay. The scholarship, along with a Myer Foundation Grant, funded a trip for him to study in England, Europe, and the USA to discover best practise. It also gave him the opportunity to exhibit his works in some of the most famous galleries and hold an exhibition at the Commonwealth Institute Art Gallery in London.

In December that year Dad, Mum, my brother and sister, and I, along with my Aunty Phil (Dad's youngest sister) packed up and went to live abroad. We left on a ship that took a month to get to London. I was eight at the time. One of the most memorable occasions on the ship was stopping off in South Africa, where we visited a tribe and were introduced to their culture, art, and animals. I was especially fascinated by the monkeys. After arriving in England, we moved into 12 Chaldon Way, Coulsdon. It was a country house on the Farthing Downs where our back gate opened onto a sea of purple flowers and little farms dotted on top of the hill. We were enrolled at the local Coulsdon Primary School close by to our home. I remember walking to school in the snow and the home cooked hot lunches we shared in the dining room every day. It was at school I met my best friend Nicola, who was the daughter of a scientist. I couldn't believe it when I went to her house and found she had a pet chimpanzee. My love for animals and the fact that I hadn't been allowed to have a dog, I thought I would try for a chimpanzee. Dad was quite firm in informing me the Government would not allow a chimpanzee into Australia. I don't take no for an answer easily, so I decided to write to the current Prime Minister of Australia, John Gorton, to ask his permission to bring a chimpanzee home. We were travelling in Europe at the time. I posted the letter with a used Norwegian stamp in Italy. Dad was convinced it had no chance of reaching its destination. After seeing how disappointed I was that I hadn't received a reply, he, with the help of my aunty, typed up a letter, signed it "John Gorton," and posted it. Although I think I was more devastated that the Prime Minister

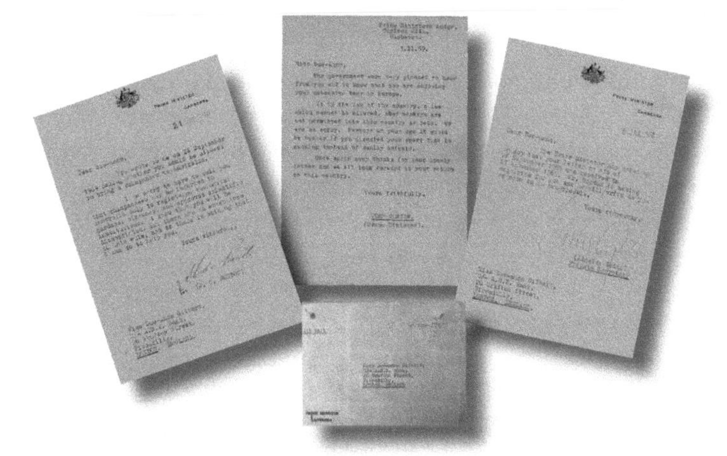

wasn't very sensitive to my needs when I read, "I think it would be more appropriate if you devoted your time to your studies instead of smelly animals." Little did Dad know there was a surprise waiting for him. Not long after arriving back in Australia, a letter addressed to me arrived with an official Australian Government emblem. Soon after, another followed. One from Andrew Peacock and another from Ainsley Gotto, on behalf of the Prime Minister. The first stated that they were considering my request, and the following informing me of the regulations, neither would work in my favour. While the three letters I received hang proudly in my office, I never got to bring the chimpanzee home, but I did end up with a dog.

My aspiration to become a teacher goes back to Grade 6 at my primary school, Mt. Clear Primary. A new teacher, Helen Button, had been posted to our school. She was very modern in her thinking, and we thought she was pretty cool. For the first time, school had become fun instead of all hard work. Funnily enough, one of my earliest memories I have from that school was in prep. A girl in the year above had fallen off the maypole and ended up with a black eye. I was too scared to look at her and pretended to be sick the next day so I didn't have to go to school.

Susie second row, second right — Brett top row, third right 1968

Then 20 plus years later, I established a charity for seriously traumatised and injured children who had far greater injuries than a black eye. However confronting it may be, I found that by looking into the eyes of children when their facial appearances had changed, some beyond recognition from burns and other injuries, you are able to see the beauty within. It was actually at Mt. Clear Primary School I first met my future husband, Brett. We were married 12 years later in 1980.

That same year, I was on my first teaching placement where I met a young girl with cigarette burns on her hands. She had been abused by a family member. In those days, such incidents were not freely talked about, but I felt it was my duty of care to engage the Childrens Protection Society and report the situation.

There was an underlying reason why I had a cause to want to follow this through and later to work with children at risk. An incident in my childhood gave me some level of understanding. This is something I have shared with very few people and I have dealt with in my own way. I made a conscious choice at that time that I was going to be a "survivor, not a victim" and that is how I got on with my life.

In 1979, I began working alongside the Childrens Protection Society while studying teaching at the Ballarat College of Advanced Education. I received this letter that read: "Her interest and enthusiasm is unusual in one so young and indicates a genuine interest in the 'at-risk' child." The experience with the Childrens Protection Society was a significant reason why I chose the path I did, dedicating my life to empower at-risk children.

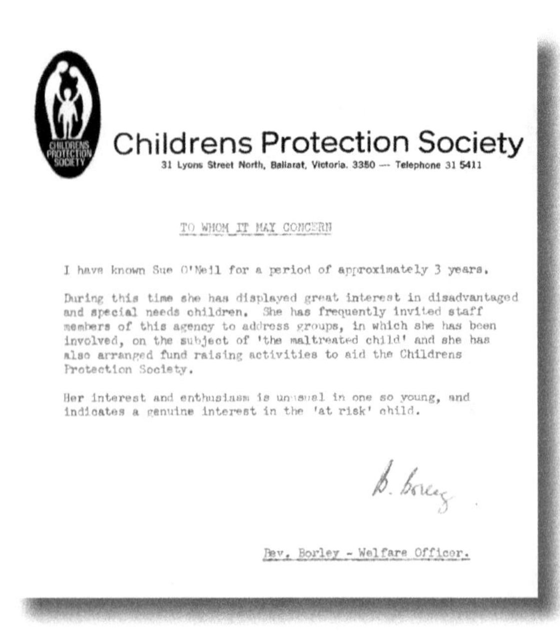

Childrens Protection Society

31 Lyons Street North, Ballarat, Victoria. 3350 — Telephone 31 5411

TO WHOM IT MAY CONCERN

I have known Sue O'Neil for a period of approximately 3 years.

During this time she has displayed great interest in disadvantaged and special needs children. She has frequently invited staff members of this agency to address groups, in which she has been involved, on the subject of 'the maltreated child' and she has also arranged fund raising activities to aid the Childrens Protection Society.

Her interest and enthusiasm is unusual in one so young, and indicates a genuine interest in the 'at risk' child.

B. Borley

Bev. Borley - Welfare Officer.

In 1981, I got my first job and began my professional career in preschool and primary school teaching. In the mornings, I was a kindergarten teacher at a neighbourhood day-care centre, and in the afternoons, I was a specialist art and physical education teacher at a private primary school. The day-care position turned out to be the most perfect job for me because Brett and I were eager to start a family, and it meant that working in a day-care centre I could take our children with me. I stayed in that position for nine years and had four beautiful children during that time - Matt in1982, Emma in 1984, Ben in 1988, and Kate in 1990.

It was here I wrote my first book titled Bruno. It was loosely based on the Elves and the Shoemaker, and the characters of the book were the children in the class. Personal computers were not around in the early 80s, they actually were not readily used in homes until 1990s. I had not learned to type, so I painstakingly scratched each letter of each word from a Letraset (dry transfer) sheet onto every page of the book.

Working in a neighbourhood day-care centre exposed me to some beautiful families but also to the dysfunction and unhealthy habits of others. The most haunting and rewarding experience I had in the nine years of teaching in the centre was meeting Will. He arrived at the centre under the watchful eye of the Department of Youth and Community Services. He had been raised in a household where both parents worked. During the day, he was contained in a cot with a bottle and watched over by two German Shepherd dogs. Will was four at the time he arrived at the centre, he couldn't walk or talk, he would curl up in the corner and hide if anyone approached him, and he was petrified of anyone in a white coat. Tears of pride poured out the day he said my name, walked along a plank, and road a trike for the first time. It was an enormous privilege that he was willing to take a chance on me as I chaperoned him in my car to dentist and doctor visits. Will would stare at me with his wide and innocent eyes. I was so proud of him and wanted to take ownership of all that he had accomplished, but the truth was he was responsible for his achievements, once he gained my trust.

Turning up to work on my first day at the Neighbourhood Centre was a little challenging when confronted with 12 little people who had a wide range of abilities. Seven children in the class had been identified as having higher than average IQ's, and several were classified as "gifted" and part of the Association for Gifted and Talented Children. Two other children had intellectual learning challenges, one had Down Syndrome. I had to put my creative thinking cap on and design a curriculum that challenged them all. The children attended kinder five days a week, as most were from homes with two working parents. Fortunately, there were a few parents in the group who were willing to offer their time and transport the children to activities outside the kinder. On Mondays and Thursdays, we had classroom activities, and Tuesdays we spent time at the Ballarat Library. On Wednesdays, we visited the Queen Elizabeth Geriatric Centre (QEGC), where the children engaged in a program I created to connect the elderly residents and the children called "Adopt a Grandparent." The elderly residents loved our weekly catch ups just as much as the children. They would dance, sing, and draw together.

Phillip

Some years later, along with Elaine, one of the mums that worked at the QEGC, we established the After School and Holiday Program on the grounds of the QEGC. It was the first after school and holiday program in Ballarat at the time. Then on Fridays, we arranged swimming lessons at a local pool. By the time the children left kinder, they all had strong water survival capabilities and could confidently swim 25 metres. One little girl, Hollie, went on to be a State Champion swimmer. The visits to the QEGC exposed the children to some wonderful characters both young and old. On one of the visits to the QEGC, we met a young man that had been "king hit" and suffered severe head and spine injuries. He became a quadriplegic, actually I think he may have been classified as a tetraplegic, a type of paralysis that affects the cervical spinal cord. The children became very fond of him so we allowed extra time to spend with him each week. He had lost his ability to talk but was able to communicate through a technical device that printed out messages. The children would eagerly stand by his wheelchair, waiting for him to send them a personal message that I would read. He had a great sense of humour and would send some funny messages that would make us all laugh.

Toward the end of my time at the Neighbourhood Centre, I developed a need to stimulate my creative brain. A friend, my mum, sister-in-law Deb, and I opened a children's store in Ballarat, which was intended as a side interest to our main jobs, but it turned into one of the biggest challenges of my life. In the store was a range of children's clothing that I designed and my mother-in-law had made originally for our children. A Melbourne agent travelling through Ballarat noticed it and made contact to ask if I was interested in selling it into a small range of boutiques. One month later, she arrived with $250,000 of orders, and I didn't know how to thread a needle on the machine. After finding a clothing manufacturing company in Avoca, a small town outside Ballarat, we produced our first range. Years later, it went into Myer, and one collection ended up as one of the most popular boys wear ranges, also the runner-up in Australian Children's Fashion Awards. Unfortunately there was a "scary" side to the industry. Besides the fact that stores were often closing down and owing money, as our range grew, we recruited companies from Melbourne to make the clothing. These companies often ran from home and garage-based workrooms, which meant going into these environments to approve the ranges. It was after the owner of one of the factories that we worked closely with was found murdered and concreted in a barrel at Pykes Creek Reservoir, that I decided it was time to get out. Two of the clothing labels were sold to Myer, and I went back to concentrating on being a mum and teacher.

I feel very adventurous. There are so many doors to be opened, and I'm not afraid to look behind them.

- ELIZABETH TAYLOR

CHAPTER TWO

Anything Is Possible

How the 'hare and turtle' story turned into the greatest funding support a charity could have wished for.

I was one of those people that was okay at most things but never really excelled in anything. I loved dancing and spent most of my time in ballet lessons growing up. My sporting abilities were especially limited. However, at uni, or teachers' college as it was called in those days, you had to select two majors. I chose art, and for some unknown reason, I took my second major in physical education. My claim to fame was a 'round off' on the beam and endurance on a run. One day, we were taken to a pine forest near a reservoir and told we were about to tackle an 8km cross country run. I had never run more than a kilometre until then. However, I did manage to keep up with some of the athletic boys and arrived back being the only female in the group. This wasn't due to natural talent but purely my determined nature and anything-is-possible attitude that had kicked in. That day, I was invited to join the early morning fitness group that met three days a week. The group was made up of about 20+ more mature professional men, a young female policewoman, our Phys.ed lecturer's wife, and me (I was only 18 at the time). Little did I know that this would come in handy years later.

It was in 1999 that Brett and my brother Simon were competing in the Australian Ironman Triathlon at Forster-Tuncurry in NSW. I remember thinking it was a ridiculous event, and wondered how anyone could possibly swim 3.8km, ride 180km, and run

42.2km, and do it in one day. I stayed to watch to the end that night and witnessed people of all abilities crossing the line; they were heroes. The crowds were still out cheering for each individual crossing the line to "You Are An Ironman." Wow! I thought, "If one could ever feel like a sporting hero, this would have to be as close as it gets." As the last competitor crossed the line, just before the cut off time of 15 and a half hours, fireworks it lit up the sky over the beach. It was then I had a crazy idea that this is something I needed do. Now at this point, I could not swim more than 25 metres, had only ever owned one bike as a child, and the endurance running that I had done in the past was a bonus. Fortunately, my father in-law Mick was a swimming coach and agreed to teach me to swim. I then went out and purchased my first road bike and became a regular at the Tann Clan running group.

In those days, a competitor had to qualify to compete in the event. I had no chance. However, there was a lottery system, so I applied and was fortunate enough to get a spot. The next year, I rocked up to Forster; there weren't many females competing in comparison to the males. The women were looked after extremely well. We had our own pre-race breakfast arranged by Glenda Baggs, who was the Administration Manager and wife of the Race Director Ken Baggs. On the course, we had our own changing facilities with cosmetics and other goodies that made each female feel so special. Race day was tough, and there was a lot of soul searching done on that 15+ hour journey. However, the finish-line was more than I could imagine. Tears were rolling down my cheeks as I approached the finish shoot. The professionals and others had gathered in the finish shoot to welcome the last few home. I was one of those, actually fifth last in a field of 1000 or more, but I felt like I had just won. I had never experienced such emotion, probably because I believed I had no athletic bones in my body, but the sheer determination and that anything-is-possible attitude got me through.

I was hooked. But it wasn't that easy to get into the event, so the following year I went to Palm Cove for a girls' trip and entered the half Ironman to attempt to gain a spot. The swim conditions were horrific, but I managed to finish. Later that night at the presentation party, and as luck would have it, my number was drawn for a place in the 2002 Ironman Australia.

That trip was also the beginning of a ten-year relationship for the KIDS Foundation with Ironman Australia. I had noticed Ironman had not aligned with a preferred charity, so some time back I had written to Glenda and sent a tape about the KIDS Foundation to see if she would pass the information onto Ken. He was apparently not one bit interested, but Glenda kept continually pestering him to look at the tape and the letter, suggesting it would be a good thing to align a charity with Ironman. It wasn't until I met Ken, that a wonderful partnership formed. He tells the story...

Post-race Ross and I went to the after party at a local resort hotel. We were enjoying the celebrations and came upon Susie and her three girlfriends who were also celebrating. Susie had just drawn the race lottery spot for the 2002 Australian Ironman Championships the following year. It wasn't long into the conversation she happened to mention the Foundation, and my response was, "So you are the Susie who Glenda has been driving me mad about." It was an opportune moment for Susie, and her request was a qualifying slot from our race, which she would raffle to raise funds for the Foundation. The rest is history as they say, but not before Ross made a magnanimous gesture with, "Go on, give her two slots!" I then had to convince Dallas O'Brien from IMG (the Ironman hosting rights) who managed the event, of the benefits of this arrangement, but they were in, and the Foundation has gone from strength to strength. It has been a good mutually benefiting relationship. Susie was able to secure Steve Moneghetti and other celebrities who are Foundation supporters to engage in the Ironman functions.

The KIDS Foundation raised well over $1.5 million dollars through the events created in association with Ironman Australia over the 10-year period until the race was bought out by an international company and the charity model changed.

Now after getting the lottery spot, the pressure was off, so I thought! Brett had gone to Shepparton to compete in a Half Ironman to qualify with a group of Ballarat triathletes. I left early after the race with Ben and Kate in their car. Coming through Bendigo, a car swerved and hit us head on. I remember waking up and seeing the car filling with smoke. I called to the kids to see if they were okay and to quickly get out, fearing the cars would burst into flames, but the doors were jammed shut and crushed from the impact. We finely wedged one open and climbed through. As it turned out, the smoke was from the airbags, and the car was not in danger of bursting into flames. Having had so many children come to the Foundation with horrific burns from car crashes, I didn't want it to be us. Standing beside the road cuddling the kids and looking at the scene was traumatic. I couldn't feel my body. It was numb, which they tell me is a sign of shock. There were car parts and Christmas presents from the other car spread all over the road. I looked at the kids to see if they were okay. They were covered in a mix of blood and gravy. We had just been to the KFC drive through in Bendigo to get lunch. Fortunately, their injuries were minor. Our car was only a month old, it was a right off, and the policeman told us later it saved our lives. All the safety features on it worked perfectly.

A friend travelling home came across the accident site and noticed my car with the bikes on the back. Knowing Brett was on his way back from Shepparton, he phoned him to let him know what to expect and that we were pretty much okay. When we left by ambulance, it looked like a disaster zone. A helicopter was called in to transport a lady from the other car. There were ambulances, police, and jaws of life. The kids were a bit bruised, and I ended up with a few broken ribs and chipped a piece of disk and bone off my lower spine. Under the guidance of a well-known surgeon, an attempt was made to treat it without major surgery. In the meantime, I could swim and ride my bike, and was under strict instruction not to run. That year, I completed the Ironman, walking the whole 42.2km, coming in seven minutes before cut-off. I did have Steve Moneghetti on track encouraging me to walk faster in fear that I was not going to make it.

A few months later, the back treatment wasn't working, so I underwent surgery to remove the fragments. I remember travelling back to Ballarat in an ambulance because I wasn't allowed to sit for some time after. That was on the Monday, and then on the Wednesday, I went to accept the Ballarat and Regional Victorian Business Women Award, standing the whole time.

Marg, Kate, Susie and Emma at the awards

WONDER WOMEN

BALLARAT AND WESTERN REGION

WOMEN IN BUSINESS AWARDS

verall winner
unded group
help children

MARIZA FIAMENGO

Star performers: The 2002 Ballarat and Western Region Woman of the Year award winner Susie O'Neill, wh won the Community, Government and Services section, front centre, is surrounded, by the winners of the sections, from left: Trainee or Apprentice, Sylvia Sweeney; Young Woman in Business, Karen Robinson, M Employee, Angela Carey; Owner/Operator, Tracey Holmes; and Indigenous Business Woman, Pauline Smit
Picture: HOLLY CURTIS

More reports an tures — Pages 2, 4 a

The following year, I met an extremely generous and "kind" man named Darren Rutherford who is the Managing Director of Giant Bicycles Australia. He had heard about my charity work and offered me the opportunity to become a Giant sponsored rider. My new bike certainly helped improve the Ironman times after that. Darren's support for his riders wasn't just about the bike, it was what went with it. He would fly to events, set up a support station, and cheer on every Giant rider until the finish, sometimes up to 16 hours, into the night. I can remember one year I was in so much pain. It had been pouring with rain, and the wet socks in the marathon leg had caused blisters the size of a half tennis ball on my feet. About 8km from the finish-line, along a stretch of road that was pitch black, with tears streaming down my face, I hear a gentle voice out of the darkness say, "How are those blisters going buddy?" I burst

Sophie and Darren

Susie and Darren

into tears, "I don't think I can do this." "Yes you can, you have never quit yet," and he handed me a clean pair of dry socks. That is one of the kindest gifts I have ever been given, one I will never forget.

Back to "loyalty, trust, and kindness," Darren is a person that has lived up to that, becoming passionate about the KIDS Foundation volunteering and fundraising. His initiatives have resulted in raising over $1.2 million dollars for the Foundation. But it's not the money that he has helped raise that makes him so special, it's the little things that he does for families that are traumatised by the most horrific injuries. Darren started donating bikes to injured children to assist in their physical mobility and recovery, and for fundraising purposes. He invited families out for meals when times were tough. He buys gifts for children and takes children and their families on outings to brighten their day. I'm so glad we were able to say thank you in a special way. In 2018, I nominated Darren for the Order of Australia, which was successful and announced in the Queen's Birthday 2020 Honours List.

After a 550-kilometre fundraising ride in 2019, we arrived at the Noosa AFL grounds to be greeted by a sea of yellow banners and flags. The big welcoming party was made up of riders' families and others attending a KIDS Foundation recovery camp who were staying nearby. A few of the young people gave heart-felt speeches of thanks to the riders. One young man named Tom, a survivor from the recovery camp spoke about a new procedure that he was hoping to have that would give him a better quality of life...

You have not lived today
until you have done
something for someone
who can never repay you.

- JOHN BUNYAN

Tom

Tom was burnt in a house fire at just three and a half months old under suspicious circumstances. He was removed from his family and soon after fostered by a beautiful lady, Dawn, who later adopted him. For the last 21 years, Tom has had over 150 surgeries and struggled with his right foot, which was partially amputated at the time of the fire. It had been suggested that having his leg amputated through a procedure called osseointegration would provide more mobility and potentially less pain. Their out-of-pocket fees were to be $35,000, and they were $23,000 short. After meeting Tom, Darren, who had literally just got off the bike, came up with an idea. He asked the group on the ride to donate $50 each to Tom's cause and in return they would receive a Giant product voucher.

The vouchers were not necessarily for the person receiving them but for them to select a young survivor attending the recovery camp to give them to. The $1,000 raised was given to Tom, who was overwhelmed. I shared this story with our other corporate partners who then wanted to help, and in one day, we had raised the money they needed to make up the shortfall. Darren's act of kindness was infectious and had flowed onto others. Tom and his mum Dawn were beside themselves to know that the life-changing surgery could go ahead, and on November 14, 2018, Tom got his new leg.

Rewind back to the Ironman story... In 2006, I was that excited to finally come in under the 14 hours, for any Ironman that is quite slow considering the champs do it in around eight hours. The bike leg did become my favourite, as the run became a walk over time. However, the 'walk-leg' became quite a profitable part of the race, bringing additional benefits to the KIDS Foundation, the principal charity for the Australian Ironman. When you walk, you get to meet some pretty special people who want to learn more about the charity. On one occasion, I walked most of the marathon with a gentleman that ended in a $150,000 sponsorship for the KIDS Foundation.

A hero is an ordinary individual who finds the strength to persevere and endure in spite of overwhelming obstacles.

- CHRISTOPHER REEVE

CHAPTER THREE

The Unsung Heroes

From the unsung heroes with big hearts and the professional athletes who thrive on the challenge of Ironman.

There are many unsung heroes that have come through Ironman. Individuals such as George Mifsud, Anthony Moustakas, Luc Evans, Brett Tynan, Christian Schwaezler, Paul Courtney, Andrew Wellington, Chris Browne, Don McKill, Leeann Llyod, Janet Miller, and many more, their partners, and families, passionate people that have been responsible for collectively, but indirectly, raising the money we have needed to support the KIDS Foundation's recovery programs.

In 2009, I received a call from an Ironman spectator who had, like many, been caught up in the emotion of the event being held at Port Macquarie. He decided he wanted to do an Ironman for a purpose and despite facing his own challenges would like to raise money for the KIDS Foundation.

His name is Brad Foster, a survivor of four brain tumours and sufferer of Retro Perennial Fibrosis, a disease that will eventually take away his sight. He had been inspired by the KIDS stories that were told on stage at the Ironman welcome nights. Brad set himself the challenge of raising $140,600, one dollar for each of the 140.6 miles it takes to complete an Ironman race. Over the next two Ironman races, he reached his target. Brad had used his profound sense of loss from his surgeries to gain his greatest sense of accomplishment. But still he wanted to do more.

There isn't a person anywhere who isn't capable of doing more than he thinks he can.

- HENRY FORD

Brad Foster - The connection to KIDS was infectious "I found a passion for a charity that has changed my life."

Brad came up with the idea that he would invite others to join him on a ride from Ballarat to Port Macquarie, approximately 1200km and with one day's rest take on the Australian Ironman Triathlon Championships. Brad's wife Annie's unwavering belief in his crazy ideas helped him believe they were possible. Brett and I, along with eight others, took on the challenge to do the ride plus the Ironman, and another 14 decided to tackle the ride. Among the group was a mutual friend, the other Susie O'Neill and her husband Cliff Farley. With support of Annie, friends, fellow triathletes, and cyclists over the following two years, Brad became the catalyst in assisting the KIDS Foundation to raise in excess of $500,000.

"There isn't a person anywhere who isn't capable of doing more than he thinks he can." – Henry Ford ...especially Brad

In 1998, I was diagnosed with a brain tumor. I flew to Sydney to meet a neurosurgeon, Dr. Bernard Kwok. He explained that I had a brain tumor the size of a lemon. The following day he performed a 13-hour operation. After being chopped from ear to ear, I survived with only the loss of my sense of smell. Although the road to recovery was hard, I had a new respect for life, "live life to the fullest."

I have regular scans to monitor the growth of the residue left after the operation. Unfortunately, the tumor began to grow again, and I had to have another operation in August 2004. The new tumor was the size of a golf ball, but this time they only had to cut half my head open. The operation took seven hours, but unfortunately Dr. Kwok was unable to get all the tumor because it was in the optic canal, so we knew it would grow back at some stage again. After a scan and checkup in March 2008, the nightmare continued. The tumor was growing again. So, in July 2008, I had my third brain operation. It took six hours following the same scar line as the first two operations. As with the previous operations, Dr. Kwok couldn't remove the whole tumor because of its critical location. This will now continue. Because of the tumor's position, it can't be removed surgically.

On September 29, 2008, I began a six-week program of radiation in Sydney in the hope that small doses of radiation over a longer period might save what sight I have left in my right eye. I was hopeful the radiation treatment would end this torment that my beautiful family and I had to endure. It has reappeared, but I take it in its stride. It has become part of my life and will one day probably take my sight.

But out of something bad there comes something good, which lead me to tackling the challenge of raising my first $140,600 for the KIDS Foundation by completing the 140.6mile Ironman race in April 2009.

Annie is his biggest supporter. She drove every kilometre of his rides and followed every step of his races. Her motivation helped him push through tough spots and tough times. Annie also became one of KIDS loyalist supporters and still is today. She heads up the catering for fundraising events, rides, and camps. In any one year, Annie and her team (Brad, Bev and John Creagh, Vanessa Moule, and Scott Diete) can prepare and serve more than 3,000 meals, saving the KIDS Foundation over $60,000 at each camp.

As his friend put it, "The challenge never seems big enough to match the courage and determination of our mate Brad." Friends have rallied around to support him. One friend donated a large billboard at the entrance of Port Macquarie that featured Brad promoting KIDS, and a bush poet wrote a poem:

And a bloke who's never quit
Is our good mate Bradley Foster.
When it comes to doing hard yards,
Brad dominates the roster.
But he's looked beyond the mirror
To find some heroes of his own
Who face their fears
and beat their nightmares,
The toughest kids he's ever known.
So, join in Brad's great mission,
Dig in deep with your donations
To help put smiles on the dials of the
children through KIDS Foundation.

By Murray Hartin

Warren Turner with Annie and Brad

Getting back to Ironman... Trying to balance being a wife, mother, and grandmother, full-time work, a PhD, and training for an Ironman was a challenge, especially when time management isn't your strongest strength. I always try to fit that extra thing in, and end up running late. My mother-in-law would often say, "I'm sure you have been born with an extra gene, Susie." My average training week was not ideal and usually ended up with something like 3km's of swimming, 200km's of riding, and at the most 20km of running, which is minimal for an Ironman.

Although I loved cycling and it was my strongest leg, it was the one that gave me the most worry. I became nervous every time I went out on the road, concerned I would have a fall or be hit by a car. We tried to find roads with minimal cars, but sometimes the random car on a country road where the driver isn't expecting cyclists is equally as dangerous. I had a rule to never go out in fog, heavy rain, and strong winds; that added to the risk.

There was one occasion a bike ride wasn't so kind to me. It was 16 hours into our dream 30th wedding anniversary trip in Bali with the whole family when the incident happened. Our accomodation was at a beautiful resort on a golf course. We woke up, had breakfast, and decided the adults would go on a guided mountain bike ride. We checked the grandchildren into kids' club and went to pick up our quite old and heavy outdated mountain bikes from resort activities. After juggling busy roads, we finally ended up on a trail through the rice paddies.

I was at the back of the pack taking in the scenery when I hit a pothole and went flying into the rice fields, tangling my leg up in the heavy bike. I knew I had hurt it badly when I saw the tibia and fibular protruding out of the unbroken skin on both sides of my ankle and the pain was unbearable. The others were far ahead and couldn't hear me calling for help, and I was sinking into the mud. Finally, they turned and realised I wasn't there and came back to find me now waist deep in the mud with the bike still tangled around my leg. Brett and the guide untangled the bike and lifted me out of the mud. They rang for the resort car to meet us at the nearest road, which was 15 minutes away by foot.

As they carried me to the car, I was silently screaming with pain, and it felt like hours. When we got back to the resort, they called for an ambulance and doctor. The doctor arrived and administered some pain killers that had little or no effect. Soon after, the ambulance, which was more like a delivery van, pulled in. On the way to the hospital, the ambulance ran out of petrol, so we stopped to fill up. Arriving at the hospital, I was taken to the emergency room, which had one bed. The X-ray showed two clean breaks in my tibia and fibular that needed pinning. There were no rods and pins that would fit my leg, so they had to have them made. Nine hours later, I went into surgery after paying $10,000 AUD upfront. The next two weeks were spent floating in a pool ring or in a wheelchair, which wasn't favourable to Kuta streets.

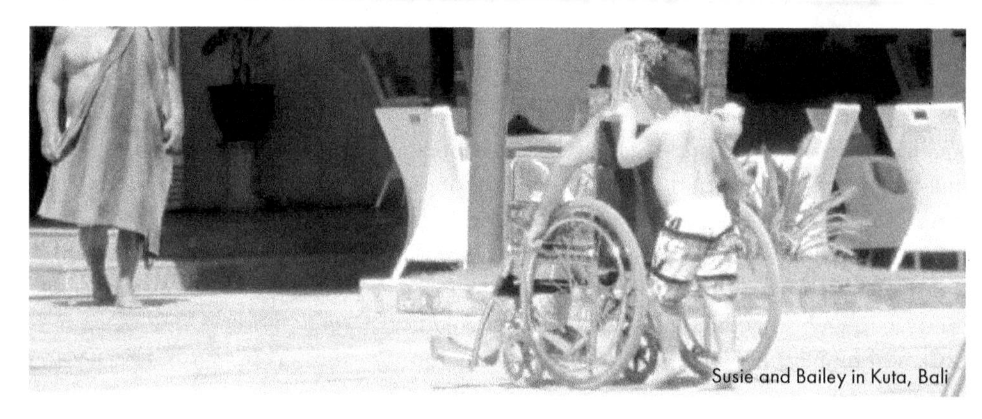
Susie and Bailey in Kuta, Bali

We had planned a special few days in the Ubud mountains to celebrate our wedding anniversary. With over 100 stairs to breakfast and cobble paths, we spent a lot of time in our room, which was fortunately quite large with a pool. Each morning a staff member would help Brett carry me down to breakfast, and if no one else was around, I would pull myself up the stairs backwards, exhausted by the time I reached the top.

Arriving back in Australia, I eventually had it checked by an orthopaedic surgeon who found another five fractures and breaks in the foot, which required a round of surgery to remove the plates and screws that were stretching and rubbing under the skin. This all happened despite the fact that I was taken to the best hospital in Bali, which was funded by the John Howard Government after the Bali bombings. The room I spent a few days in after surgery was more like a luxury suite with a marble lined bathroom, and the nursing care was exceptional.

Fortunately, other than a few falls at the beginning, I've never had another serious fall off my road and race bikes. Funnily enough, running caused the most injuries and the biggest fall—tripping on a pothole in the dark and breaking my little finger. My finger was sidewards coming out of my glove. I had an excruciating 3km walk to get home to get the car and drive to hospital. The physician put the splint on crookedly, and it never returned to its normal shape, permanently bent. Until well into my 40's, other than a scalded foot as a baby, I had never experienced hospital life other than to give birth. But then it came thick and fast with the car accident, this Bali bike accident, open heart surgery, the broken finger, a shoulder reconstruction, and knee surgery all before I was 60.

Now, back to Ironman again, a special year was in 2008 when the whole six O'Neill family members completed the Australian Ironman Championships at Port Macquarie. Fortunately, our children were given my husband's athletic ability, and a couple went on to be Australian champions in their age groups. After 12 consecutive Ironman Australia finishes and one Melbourne Ironman, things came to a halt for me. One day riding the Great Ocean Road with my doctor, I happen to mention that my heart rate in training had been higher than normal. Due to family history and as a precautionary measure, he sent me to a cardiologist. After several tests, the results came back fine, but unrelated a small 4mm tumour was found on the aortic valve. The doctors were reassuring me not to worry about it as I was probably born with it and it wasn't dangerous until it reached 1cm. Six months later, tests revealed the tumour had grown to over 1.5cm and required open heart surgery. This was eight weeks before the 2013 Ironman. That year I was a spectator and got to put medals around the finisher's necks and share in their excitement. I thank Ironman and training using a heart rate monitor as saving my life. The tumour looked like a balloon hanging from a string and fell off in the surgery. This meant it probably was not long from falling off naturally and would have resulted in blocking the artery. This also meant that the tumour didn't get to pathology to find out if it was benign or malignant, so I continue to have scans every 12 months. At the time, I was told this operation was quite rare as these tumours are usually found in autopsies. I did actually secretly plan my own funeral, but was so glad it was not needed. Rehab and the post-surgery recovery went quite well due to my fitness. So well in fact that I got to walk the Coast to Coast in England and ride across Italy with friends three months later and then compete in the 70.3 World Championships in Las Vegas, six months after the surgery.

Emma, Ben, Kate, Susie, Brett and Matt

In 2015, I competed in my 16th and 15th Ironman at Forster/Port Mac. It was one of my proudest days to have the whole family standing at the finish line. The six O'Neills and Kate's now husband Ricky came together to do what was expected to be my last Ironman. Then I was granted a legacy spot to do my dream race - the Ironman in Kona, Hawaii. My Ironman story was to continue...

Susie and Brett

Mike Riley and Susie

Nellie

In 2017, I headed off to the World Championships in Hawaii. I loved every minute of that race, even the excruciating pain that happened in parts, the heat, and the loneliness in the pitch-black dark stretches in the marathon leg, but it was one of the best days of my life and ran true to "anything is possible." Share one dinner with the O'Neills and you will know the apples don't fall far from the tree, but still it's their choice when it came to triathlons and Ironman.

Dave Orlowski with Brock

Chrissy Wellington
with Amanda, Chris, Brittney and Matt

Ironman and its community introduced many individuals who thrive on the challenge of this unique sport to the KIDS Foundation. They became ambassadors and fundraisers, some from afar like Chrissy Wellington from the UK, a four-time Ironman Triathlon World Champion. Another was the generous spirited Dave Orlowski from the U.S. Dave was one of the fifteen that tackled the first ever Ironman race in 1978. He placed third wearing cut off jeans and a borrowed bike. At the time, he was a young Marine and did it for the "free food and beer" at the end. Sadly, Dave passed away after a long, hard battle with leukemia in December 2020. Dave joined us on the 2010 KIDS 1200km ride and then completed the Ironman.

Both Chrissy and Dave raised quite a lot of money for the KIDS Foundation encouraging fellow triathletes and mates from their hometowns to donate. There have been other amazing ambassadors that have come through Ironman and Ironman-related events such as actor Dan McPherson and Craig "Crowie" Alexander, an Australian triathlete and the 2008, 2009, and 2011 Ironman Triathlon World Champion. By winning his third Hawaiian Ironman World Championship, he also claimed a new world record time and was crowned "King of Kona."

Along with wife Neri and friend John Minto, Craig has worked tirelessly for the KIDS Foundation for more than 15 years. They have attended camps and raised much needed funds. Sometimes it is difficult to know who inspires who at the KIDS Foundation.

There is a special bond between our Ambassadors and the children. It may even have to do with the fact that like Craig, children recovering from severe burn and injury trauma know all about facing repeat painful challenges. Physical toughness is equal to the mental strength that enables them to get through.

*Life is very interesting.
In the end, some of your
greatest pains become
your greatest strengths.*

- DREW BARRYMORE

Craig Alexander

I first met Susie O'Neill nearly 15 years ago at Ironman Australia in Port Macquarie. Susie was racing, along with many others including her family, to raise funds and awareness for the KIDS Foundation. I was an event Ambassador for Ironman Australia, and the KIDS Foundation was the official charity partner aligned with the event. After our initial meeting, Susie approached me with the idea of becoming a KIDS Foundation Ambassador. She told me all about the charity, its origins, and goals. Her passion for these children and their families was totally evident and infectious. She had a clear vision of where help was needed and how to help, as well as a relentless desire to raise awareness around preventing such injuries. Susie had this way of connecting with children and families at their darkest times, understanding their needs and where they were at in the lifelong rehabilitation process. I think her background in teaching and creative thinking was instrumental in being ahead of the game in programs and ideas.

Susie is a real progressive thinker and finds a way to do the impossible. She never lets the kids down, finding ways to fulfil their wishes, helping them settle back into school, or find work, or rebuild their home life physically and emotionally. Her personality and passion for the work done by the KIDS Foundation has been influential in attracting many high-profile ambassadors and patrons to bring publicity to the cause. I was actually at a fundraising event when Susie was introduced to Scott Morrison, who at the time was the Member for Cook. They instantly connected and chatted over coffee about their common interest in supporting troubled youth.

Susie is the sort of person that doesn't ask anyone to do anything she wouldn't do herself, to the extent of riding a bike 1,200km and then doing an Ironman after one day's rest. At the time, KIDS Foundation had a great partnership with Giant bikes that sponsored their fundraising cycling events. A group of 40+ cyclists, which included the General Manager of Giant, Darren Rutherford, who also had a personal passion for KIDS, rode from Melbourne to the Ironman in Port Macquarie. I joined in on day seven of their ride. It was actually the last day, and we rode into the town led by a fire truck to a group of waiting supporters and media there to welcome us in.

Ride to Port 2012

I have also had the privilege of seeing first-hand on many occasions the huge impact the KIDS Foundation makes. I have attended camps, met the courageous children, survivors, and the families involved with the Foundation, and played a small part in raising funds at much needed times. The KIDS Foundation is an incredible organisation whose impact on thousands of children and their families is immeasurable. Susie is definitely one of a kind!"

Matt, Craig and Kel

Ride to Port 2012

Susie and Greg

My passion for the KIDS Foundation has been instrumental in attracting many high-profile ambassadors and patrons but only ones that I admire for who they are, "good" people, not necessarily their status. Good people, it comes back to "trust, loyalty, and kindness" that matters.

Our Ambassadors and Patrons of the Foundation get to share occasions with the most courageous and inspirational young people, and we want them to also be inspired by role models that represent the Foundation.

The greatness of a community
is most accurately
measured by the compassionate
actions of its members.

- CORETTA SCOTT KING

The Hon. Scott Morrison MP
"Considering my profile is not that high..."

It was at a fundraising event on December 15, 2012 that I was introduced to Scott Morrison and we chatted about our work with at-risk young people. He invited me to his office in Cronulla the next time I was to come to Sydney to view some of the opportunities he had given young people in his region.

It was in about February 2013 after quite a bit of research with Cronulla residents that I wrote to Scott Morrison and expressed my enthusiasm for him to accept an invitation to become Parliamentary Patron of the KIDS Foundation. I felt his family and community values and his desire to build capacity to address the many challenges communities face aligned with the core values of the KIDS Foundation. He accepted. Unbeknown to us, he had done quite a lot of research on the KIDS Foundation as well. On March 21, 2013 Scott Morrison made a speech in Parliament recognising the work of the KIDS Foundation. He delivered a much-detailed transcript on the organisation to members of Parliament. The information he provided was precise and nicely captured our work and programs.

The unexpected open-heart surgery put my travelling back a little and accepting the invitation to meet Scott and his team. Finally, I got to go to Sydney in June and scheduled a meeting with Scott at his offices. Walking into his office, I knew straight away we had made a good choice by engaging Scott in this way. Hanging proudly on the wall of his office are photos of groups of young people of all nationalities. In one photo, Scott and the Labour MP Jason Clare are pictured walking the Kokoda Trail with a group of young people. They included surf lifesavers from the Cronulla shire and young people from the Muslim community in Bankstown. Another photo captures Scott, Jason, and MP Rob Oakeshott, along with a group of young people from each of their electorates. The multicultural group included young people from indigenous African and Muslim backgrounds, as well as from Cronulla. They had retraced the steps of Australian prisoners of war on the Sandakan death march, through the jungles of Borneo.

We chatted about the work of the Foundation, and I have etched in my mind when he said, "Considering my profile is not that high, it may be worth also inviting a sitting Labour Member to accompany me in my role." At the time, as well as being the Federal Member for Cook, Scott Morrison was the Shadow Minister for Immigration & Citizenship/Shadow Minister for Productivity and Population. We never got around to putting this in place as Tony Abbott went on to lead the Coalition to victory and become the Prime Minister of Australia a few months later on September 18, 2013. And, from there, the rest is history. But I do remember exactly where I was on the August 24, 2018, driving to Melbourne airport the back way from Ballarat, along Plumpton Road, when I heard on the radio that Scott Morrison was the new Prime Minister, and I shed a tear. So, the 'not so high-profile' politician went on to became the most high-profile politician in our country. On the KIDS 25th Anniversary, we received an unexpected surprise when a video clip arrived from the PM speaking the words:

As a Dad, to be honest, I wish that we didn't need a KIDS Foundation, because then our kids would be living happy, healthy, and care-free lives, there'd be no risk, but we know that is not true, so that is why I'm thankful there is a KIDS Foundation. I know as you do, that life throws its curve balls and you support the families when they face their worst. I honour the work of the KIDS Foundation, that they do every day, that you do every day, in support of children living with burns or serious injury. This is demanding work, and I'm in awe of what you do, and importantly you are there to do your part to prevent these injuries as well. So, on this 25th anniversary, I want to thank you for all of your efforts, and I want to wish you the best for the next 25 years as well. You are there when people need you most. That is what being a mate is all about, that is what being an Australian is all about. Thank you."

The Hon. Scott Morrison MP

Scott Morrison has certainly entered into one of the most challenging times in politics with the coronavirus pandemic and the impact it has had on changing the way we live. As much as it was the toughest time many had experienced, we were given something some of us regularly experience freely - "TIME." For many of us, we didn't have to be anywhere at any certain time, at any certain moment. Looking around, we could see inspiration everywhere, people finding their best self and learning from others. We did the same at KIDS. We took time to create, be inspired, and become the best support service for our educators, families, and children. It also made us realise that much of what we do in life is a privilege.

Be yourself;
everyone else
is already taken.

- OSCAR WILDE

Madame Butterfly

The other Susie O'Neill - A common cliche' in my life is "you have a famous name, can you swim?"

The ways in which our Ambassadors have come to the Foundation have often been "we were destined to meet" scenarios. It is pretty beneficial having the same name as Susie O'Neill, the former Olympic swimmer (Madame Butterfly). I first met Susie in 1995. My youngest daughter had entered a competition to have a swimming lesson with Susie O'Neill. Her entry was based on the fact that her mother had the same name. We met again through a Telstra donation about eight years later and then again in 2010 though our mutual friend Brad. We have been friends with Susie and her husband Cliff ever since. Along with our husbands, we have a love for triathlons and Ironman events.

Funnily enough, sometimes Brett and I end up with the upgrade, even flowers and fruit in our room on one occasion. When we did a team event, guess who did the swim? The bike leg is my favourite, and neither of us enjoy the run, so it was a toss of the coin! One year we searched for another Susie O'Neill that had the same name and spelling, and could run, thinking it would be fun to have the three Susie's to tackle the half Ironman event in Cairn's. We actually did find another Susie who was a real estate agent, but unfortunately, she injured her leg and couldn't run. So that time Susie (Madame Butterfly) lost the flip of the coin and got to do the run.

Brett, Susie, Susie and Cliff

The day of the race was taken very casually and turned out to be quite eventful. Standing in the viewing area cheering our team mates on, a whisper was going around about the boat to the left keeping an eye on the territorial crocodile and another further out, on a shark. While I was concerned for Susie, I was certainly glad I wasn't in that water. The fact that the race was not stopped, and competitors remained in the water, gave us some comfort that the danger was minimal, but I was still relieved it wasn't me. As expected, Susie was one of the first out of the swim and handed the chip to me, and I went off to tackle the bike leg. We had given each other a window of expected times; however, our predictions were a little out. I arrived back to the change point over ten minutes earlier than expected, and Susie wasn't anywhere to be seen. So, the event volunteers went in search and found her chatting to some fans in the back corner. Eventually, dreading this leg, Susie left to tackle the 21km run in what had developed into a hot afternoon. The riders were required to catch a bus back to the finish line where you ran through with your teammates. By the time the bus arrived back, Susie had completed the run in a ripper-time, and I didn't make it back and missed finishing with her. Then to top it off, we missed the presentation. Not thinking we had placed, we were surprised when the officials found us sometime later and presented us with medals for taking out second place.

Susie and Susie

Susie, Susie and Cliff

There have been a few funny occasions where despite the fact there is quite a few years difference in age and height, I have been mistaken for Madame Butterfly. One was with Ken Morgan at the Australia Day Finalist official presentations where he announced to the other recipients and guests that he had a pair of my bathers framed and hanging proudly in his living room (that would not be a pretty picture).

Alex, Susie and Susie

Another with Denise Drysdale at a function in an aged care centre where in her speech she gave the guests a run-down on my Olympic Medals and history and then went on to offer swimming lessons to the aged care residents. At that point of time, I was still learning to swim myself. One other very embarrassing time was when I was sitting in the Green Room ready to go on a midday TV show and they were running a series of promos on Susie's achievements. The assistant producer would have been pulled over the coals for that one!

Susie would have to be one of the most genuine and grounded people I have ever met. An article in the Daily Telegraph (July 2014) read, "Don't think you're better than anyone else because you can swim fast—is how Susie O'Neill's dad kept Golden Girl grounded," which pretty much says it all. Susie said she never felt her parents loved her more because she was good at swimming and that her brother and sister were treated just the same.

If you could choose one characteristic that would get you through life, choose a sense of humour.

- JENNIFER JONES

Denise Drysdale

I have met some very special people in some of the most unexpected circumstances. There is a saying I stand by that - when you give, you receive ten-fold. That is how I met one beautiful person. I was on a plane returning to Melbourne seated in the front row and hadn't taken notice of the lady sitting beside me. The hostess came around to take our order. The person beside me was foraging around in her bag for her purse for a few loose coins to purchase a wine, but was having trouble finding it. I got my money out (in the days when you could pay with money) and said, "Let me shout you a drink and I'll have one too." I looked over and it was none other than Denise Drysdale. We started chatting, and I was telling her how I used to do an "accident story segment" on her co-star's show that Ernie Sigley hosted and filmed out of BTV-6 Ballarat and all the funny stories that happened behind the scenes. My acting and singing talents didn't quite match that of Denise's, so there was never a "Hey Paula" famous moment. We then got onto why I was on the plane, which was returning from a meeting to do with the KIDS Foundation. When it was time to exit the plane, Denise handed me a piece of paper with her phone number and said, "Call me if you ever want me to do something for the Foundation." That was back in about 2000, and in 2003, I did call her and ask if she would be an Ambassador for our Connecting Generations program, "Adopt a Grandparent." I invited her to speak at a function in Geelong to launch the program and played a video that showcased the work of the KIDS Foundation. Denise was to follow. It is not often Denise is speechless, but on this occasion, the tears streaming down her face prevented her from breaking into one of her hilarious talks. However, she did pull through and delivered a more than expected presentation, which was always the case.

Brock and Denise

Over the past 17 years, Denise has travelled to all parts of Australia hosting, emceeing, and just making people laugh for the KIDS Foundation. She has this magical way of convincing a donor to double his pledge and made our events something to remember, just by her being there. Denise is a loveable and special person within the KIDS Foundation family.

I love Susie for the person she is so kind and caring, she really loves those kids. Her unexpected health problems did not stop her dedication to her work for the Foundation, she gives 100%. The children, Susie, and her team support are amazing. Their stories break your heart and bring you to tears. We have had lots of fun together, and I love working with her. One time we had an event I was hosting for the Foundation "Dine in White," everyone turned up in white, which I guess you do when you "dine in white". I turned up in my floral dress. Susie forgot to tell me I had to wear white. The letter did say … "dine in white," maybe a "Ding Dong" moment. But I fixed that. The Foundation were selling dressing gowns with vouchers in the pockets as part of their fundraising and they happened to be white. So, I wore a dressing gown for most of the night. I felt right at home snuggled up in my gown and raised a bit of money, selling out all the dressing gowns.

Dine In White 2018

Matt and Denise

There have been some pretty talented artists that have drifted into the life of the KIDS Foundation, like Jimmy Barnes and his children the "Tin Lids," Mahalia, Eliza-Jane "E.J.," Jackie, and Elly-May. There was a connection with the Foundation in that E.J. had received burns from a boiling cup of tea given to her by an air hostess on a plane while Jane and Jimmy slept. On arrival, she was taken to hospital with severe burns. The Tin Lids were an Australian children's pop group formed in 1990. Jane and Jimmy wrote a song "Calling Kids" for the Foundation. On several occasions, I got to visit their home, which had a recording studio, to hear updates of the song. One time, my husband came along with me the same day the water dispenser in their fridge broke. Brett, being a plumber, fixed it for them, his little claim-to-fame moment. The Tin Lids

John and Susie

performed the song at a function we had at the Grand Hyatt in Melbourne in 1993. At the same event, Peter Andre and Richard Clapton donated their time to perform. Another special Ambassador we had in the 90s for the KIDS Foundation was John Farnham. He wrote (with the help of friend Tony Healy) a regular article for our KIDS' magazine, "Kelly St." Tony Healy was responsible for bringing many opportunities to KIDS like meeting Niki Lauda. Another connection with our burn survivors, Niki Lauda was attempting to win his second F1 world title when his Ferrari hit a bank at high speed and caught fire during the 1976 German Grand Prix. He was taken to hospital and treated for severe burns, but not expected to live. His mental strength was what gave him what he needed to survive. One ear had been so badly burnt it required surgery to rebuild it, but he rejected this idea, because he didn't want to waste time in getting back in the cockpit. I believe six weeks after the accident he was back in his Ferrari, with bandaged wounds. Through Tony, Niki Lauda donated the Lauda Air Corporate box at the Grande Prix in Melbourne each year for several years. Not only were we given the Friday to run a fundraiser from his box, but it led to running a "Celebrity Billycart Race" on the track, with many more high-profile Ambassadors, Danny Frawley, Nick Green, Drew Ginn, and Steve Moneghetti, just to name a few. Some whose devotion to KIDS continues today, like Steve Moneghetti.

Jamie Durie, Kate Kendall, Susie O'Neill, Danny Frawley and Krista Vendy

*I look for these qualities
and characteristics in people.
Honesty is number one, respect,
and absolutely the third
would have to be loyalty.*

- SUMMER ALTICE

Steve Moneghetti

Back in 1993 I approached Steve Moneghetti to become our first ambassador for the KIDS Foundation. Steve, is an Australian long-distance runner and Commonwealth Games Gold medallist, who was born and still lives in my hometown, Ballarat, Victoria. Since retiring in 2000 he has remained involved in sport as a former Chair of the VIS, Chef de Mission of Commonwealth Games Teams and is currently a Board Member of Sport Australia and Commonwealth Games Australia. Steve was awarded an AM for 'significant service to Athletics as a marathon runner, administrator and mentor to young athletes'. His loyalty to KIDS and the cause stands true today, accepting some very different challenges along the way.

Lee Troop, Greg Stewart, Steve Moneghetti and the cycling team

One year we came up with a fundraising idea of doing an Ironman team event from Ballarat to Forster Tuncurry, approximately 1300km. We had Susie Maroney OAM completing the 4km swim leg, Greg Stewart, IM triathlete and his mates, the 180km cycle leg, with Steve Moneghetti and Lee Troop completing 42.2km marathon each day, over six days. Our biggest challenge was to a find pool for the swim leg in the small towns we were planning to stop at along the way. Taking the "anything is possible" attitude, we decided to put a pool on the back of a truck. Michael Thorpe generously donated his truck and time to make this happen.

Susie Maroney OAM

Each morning the local Fire Brigade's would fill it and once the swim was completed, empty it back into the tank to recycle. The pool on the back of a truck became popular and attracted quite a lot of media attention.

Steve is the longest serving Ambassador for the KIDS Foundation. For 28 years he has been an active speaker at events and fundraising functions, attended school presentations and participated in a number of our media and promotional events.

I have loved my role as Ambassador of the KIDS Foundation. It certainly has been a long run starting way back when the Foundation was first established. I was inspired by Susie O'Neill's vision initially and have been amazed ever since by her passion and determination to make the lives of children and young people better ... happy, healthy, and safe you might say!

As a former teacher and now a person heavily involved in community life, it is so good to see first-hand the work done by Susie and her team, and I can say unreservedly that they are making a significant difference not only at a local level but Australia wide.

I have always believed that one person can make a difference and Susie is certainly that ONE person! If you were going to live your life following a motto then "trust, loyalty, and kindness" would be a pretty good one to use.

There is only one better feeling than waking up wanting to make a difference today and that is resting your head on the pillow knowing that you have. People might talk about it, but Susie just gets on and makes it happen.

The choices you make now,
the people you surround
yourself with, they all have
the potential to affect your life,
even who you are, forever.

- SARAH DESSEN

CHAPTER FOUR

What you do with what you have and the choices you make guide the path that leads you to where you are going.

Back tracking to the 1980s, it was an experience at the aged care centre that I took my kindergarten children to, to adopt their grandparent, that led me to establishing a foundation. There was a 12-year-old boy who was actually sleeping in a ward with three gentlemen in their 90s, which wasn't a healthy environment for a young person to be in. At the time, there were no rehabilitation centres that catered for children. I went home very disturbed and told Brett, who is a tradie, the story. I wanted to create a child-friendly space, so he agreed to help raise some money and get his tradie mates to also help. It was at this time in 1993 that I decided to establish the Foundation to try to get what we needed donated. We were allocated an old dining room within the grounds of the aged-care facility to renovate. A few years later when it was time to commence the build, the government provided a refurbishment grant, which meant the whole facility was going to be upgraded and our money could be directed towards obtaining better equipment and facilities for the children.

Eventually in 2000, the KIDS Foundation, being integral in the process, officially opened one of the first children's rehabilitation units in regional victoria, named "Pete's Place," at the Queen Elizabeth Centre in Ballarat. Today it is used by more than 600 children each year for day therapies as well as for the occasional stay. Years later, due to the many families of children who had suffered burns and were seeking support, the Foundation established the Burn Survivors' Network, which was incorporated into the Injury Recovery program. The term "survivor" is important and reflects the philosophy of what we practise at KIDS, which we believe empowers the healing process.

The new complex took several years to build and was opened in stages. It was extremely rewarding and exciting to walk into the official opening of the child-friendly Pete's Place at the Queen Elizabeth Centre in 2000. Olympians Nick Green and Julianne Adams were part of the official opening.

Nick and Julianne

KIDS Foundation

Our mission is to ensure that every child is safe - free from injury and harm.

We aim to keep children safe and create a better life for those living with serious trauma, harm, injury, and burns.

Our prevention programs educate and empower children to build a strong sense of identity and wellbeing so that they can keep themselves and others safe while still allowing them to be kids. Educating children through the SeeMore Safety Program is our focus.

Our recovery programs support children with horrific injuries and trauma caused by burns, accidents, dog attacks, crime, neglect, abuse, and environmental events. We deliver injury recovery camps, leadership workshops, and the National Burn Survivors' Network.

Our advocacy work gives children a voice and agency in their own learning. We empower them to build self-worth, wellbeing, respectful relationships, values, and behaviours that allow them to become responsible risk takers and contributors to society.

Every day the team at the KIDS Foundation devotes time and resources to empowering and educating children and their families on ways to prevent injuries and trauma associated with events that put children in dangerous situations. That is how KIDS gets its acronym "Kids In Dangerous Situations."

KIDS Foundation exists because 35,000 children in Australia will go to a hospital emergency department each week due to injury. More than twice the number of hospital admissions for illness and disease combined, every year. However, injury does not receive the same attention or financial assistance that curing disease and illness does.

No matter what sort of difficulties,
how painful the experience is,
if we lose our hope,
that's our real disaster.

- DALAI LAMA XIV

Tye

The first person to stay in the facility was Tye, a young 14-year-old boy from a regional Victorian town who had survived a fire incident, and was left with horrific burns.

For Tye, it started off like any ordinary school day. He woke up, put on his shorts and beloved basketball singlet, and took off for his early morning run, up and down the steep streets of Daylesford. But it was colder than usual, and when Tye returned home, he turned on the gas heater, lay down in front to warm up, and fell asleep. Something he says he had never done before. When he woke, he found himself on fire. "I just raced outside and rolled around on the grass. It saved my life," he said. His mother, who had been asleep, heard his screams and ran to help. "One of his arms was completely black," she said. Tye spent several months in The Royal Children's Hospital Melbourne, three weeks in intensive care and the rest rehabilitating, with burns to 30% of his body. His weight plummeted from 60 to 40 kilograms, and it was six weeks before he began to walk again. His neck was supported by a brace for many months as it took a long time for his muscles to regain their strength. He wore pressure garments from his chin down to his waist to try to reduce scarring around his skin grafts. Tye was a basketball fan, and his most enjoyable moment while recovering in hospital was a visit from his basketball heroes, Andrew Gaze and Leonard Copeland. Survivors left with severe burn injuries often describe the recovery as extremely painful and somewhat agonising. Tye developed a disheartening approach to physio, baths, and broken grafts, which he says has left him with terrifying memories.

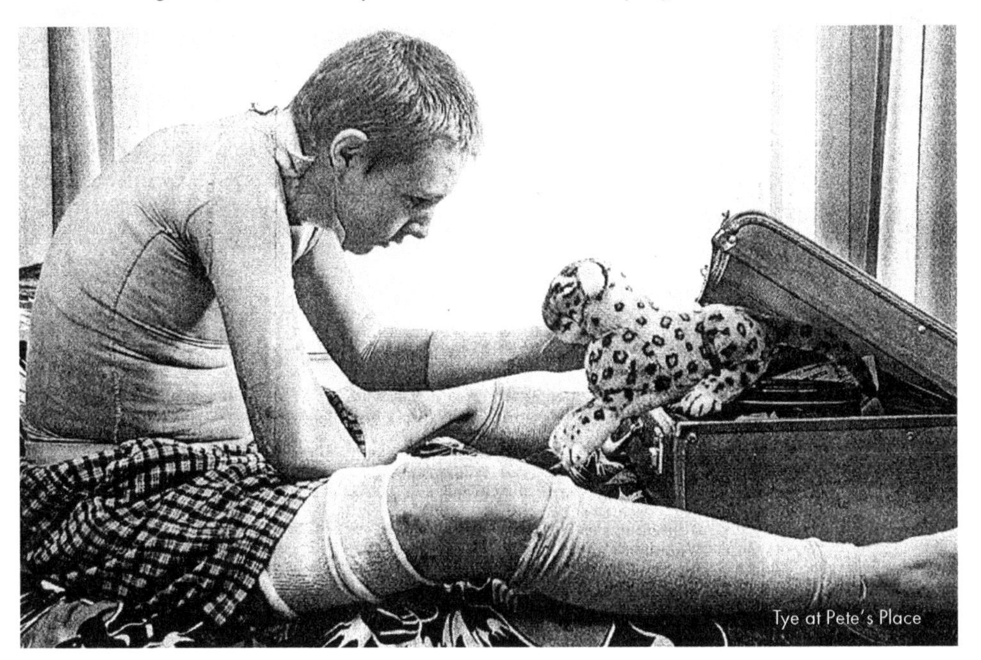

Tye at Pete's Place

"It wasn't until I moved to Pete's Place that I started to feel like I might be okay and get back to some sort of normal life. My room was pretty cool. It looked like a bedroom rather than a hospital. There was a TV, computer, games, and special physiotherapy equipment to help with my treatment. The rooms had really good sound proofing so friends and my mum could visit, and we could play music," said Tye.

Having a teaching background allowed me the opportunity to spend some time helping Tye with his schoolwork. When it was time for Tye to return home, we searched for programs to support children like Tye who had survived burn injuries and the trauma that goes with it. We found most were tied to the hospital systems, which for some young people were not what they needed.

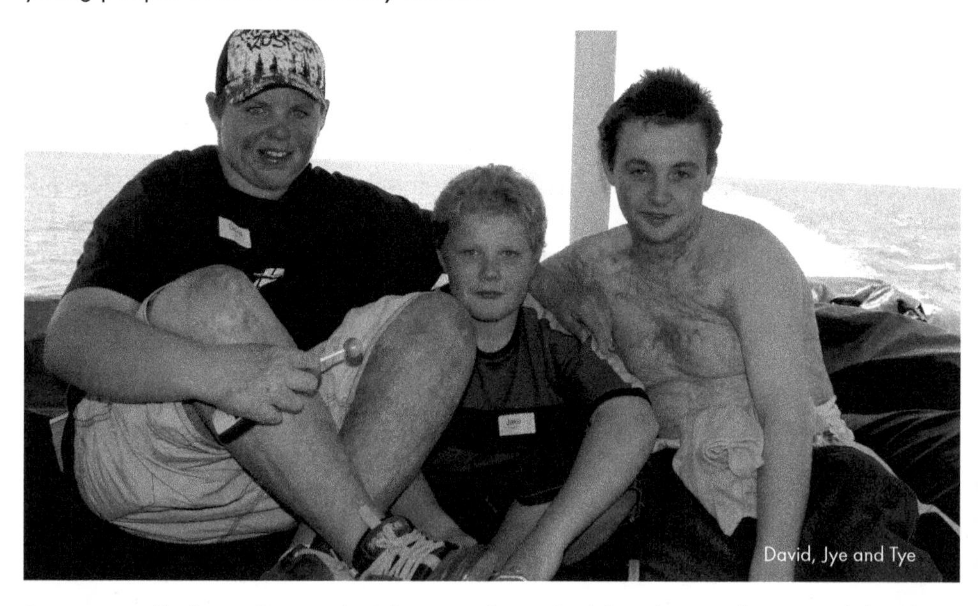
David, Jye and Tye

Survivors will often tell you what they need is to feel they have a future and that there is hope that they can overcome the painful situation that life has dealt them. There is usually a hard road ahead to recovery for these kids, and often it can be as traumatic as the incident that changed their life, usually in a split second. For children that survive a burn injury, it is the baths and the ongoing surgeries to release the skin and grafts that is what they talk about most. They need support to help them find the courage and strength they found to survive the horrific experience in the first place and regain confidence to do things they did in their life before the incident.

It wasn't long after Tye returned home from Pete's Place that we saw a Channel 7 current affair program on the television about a hospital-initiated retreat for burn survivors being held in NSW. They were short of funds to run it and were searching for donors. We had a few thousand dollars left from Pete's Place, so we contacted them, and long story short, decided to donate it to the program and to take Tye and other Victorian survivors along with us. The cost to fly was far too expensive, so we boarded a train and headed on a long journey to NSW.

Amanda and Susie

If one suffers we all suffer.
Togetherness is strength.
Courage.

- JEAN-BERTRAND ARTISTIDE

Amanda

The pain a mother feels.

We had been introduced to Andy, a young man that had suffered horrendous burns, by Dr. Sally Cockburn, known as Dr. Feelgood. His burns caused severe damage to his legs and feet and the ability to walk. Andy was under the care of Dr. Feelgood who generously gave her time and came along with us to provide medical support. It made such a difference to everyone on that trip to have an extremely knowledgeable medical practitioner and a person with great humour. Also on the train with us was a little four-year-old girl Amanda that won our hearts, and her mum Elizabeth, who in 2008 writes to thank us and tells her story...

It was a pleasant April's day. Kevin, my husband, and my eldest son Brendan went for a drive over to Kev's mother's place. My other son Raymond was across the lake at my mothers. I was outside doing the washing, and my little girl Amanda was handing me the pegs and chatting away to me, "Mummy, can I please bring my doll and pram outside to play?" she asked. I told her that she could go and get them, and I went on doing the washing. Some time went by, and I heard her screaming. I dropped what I was doing and ran to see what was wrong. Not knowing what to expect, as I was coming in the door, she was coming out of the kitchen door. I stopped dead. Amanda was covered in flames. I got her and rolled her on the ground. I then rang my mother to ask her to take us to the hospital, as Amanda has been burnt. When my mum and dad arrived, they took one look at her and then dad grabbed the hose and hosed her down as her clothes were still smouldering. Mum was on the phone ringing for an ambulance. That was when I lost it and went to pieces. Dad stood out at the front so that the ambulance knew where to come. When they arrived, they started to cut her clothes off her. Amanda was screaming, "Take me to the doctors, it hurts when I breath."

We were rushed into Horsham to Wimmera Base Hospital. While we were in emergency, I looked away while they were working on her. Amanda said, "Look at me mummy." From that moment, I hated myself. The doctor rang the Royal Children's Hospital in Melbourne and was talking to them for a while. When he came back, he said that she had to go to Melbourne and asked if I would be going with her. "Of course, I am going with her," I answered. So, we were air lifted to the Royal Children's Hospital. Kev said he would drive down but would go home first and pack a case for me. We were in Melbourne within an hour. Kev arrived about five hours later. The staff were waiting for us and so was my sister-in-law, Jenny. We were taken straight up to the burns unit and into a room that had a huge bath. They unbandaged Amanda so that the doctors could see her burns. Amanda was burnt from her chest to her knees. They said that they would give her a special bath the next day. Amanda was lying there in her bed all bandaged up with drips in her arms and a tube up her nose, and she was in a lot of pain. How could I have let this happen to my baby girl? She was only four years old. The next morning it was time for her bath. They laid her on a bed and then lowered her down into a huge bath. When Dr. Keogh, the doctor who would look after Amanda, told me that they would have to do skin grafts, I told him to use my skin as she had been through enough. Dr. Keogh told me that they could not use my skin; they had to use her skin. That made me hate myself even more because there was nothing I could do to help ease her pain. Amanda was afraid and scared as she was in a strange place with strangers all around her taking blood, giving her medicine, and taking her temperature and her blood pressure. She had enough and told them to go away and leave her alone.

For the first two weeks, I stayed in the room with her. I couldn't sleep at night and watched her as she lay there, knowing that I couldn't do anything for her. The hatred I had toward myself grew stronger and stronger. A nurse came in and said that they had arranged for a social worker to come and see me. David was a terrific person. He tried to help me. He asked how it happened, and I told him that I was doing the washing, and while I was out at the wash line, Amanda had climbed up on the cupboard and got a lighter and was playing with it when her clothes caught alight. David told me that it was not my fault and that accidents happen. That still didn't make me feel any better about myself.

Amanda went for her first lot of skin grafts. When I was called to go into the recovery room to her, I freaked out because she had a blood transfusion. I asked them what had gone wrong. They told me that everything went well and that it was normal. They told me that some people need blood after having grafts. So, I then asked them if the blood was free of any disease. They reassured me that it was. David, the social worker, got me a room across the road at the Ronald McDonald House. Every time someone walked into Amanda's room, she would tell them to go away, she wanted to be left alone. So, I decided that I would help the nurses with Amanda's care. I helped with her baths, helped to take her temperature and blood pressure, and helped to give her medicine. For the next seven weeks, Amanda had skin grafts three days a week. I felt my whole life was over and my world came crashing down around me. After seven weeks, Amanda was discharged. We were only home two weeks when Amanda was back in hospital. What sort of a mother was I to have let this happen to my little girl?

After Amanda was discharged this time, we had to go to the Royal Children's Hospital every three months. On one of our outpatient visits, Jane Bartlett, the physiotherapist that was measuring Amanda for her special suits said that she put Amanda down to go on a burns camp if I was interested. I talked to Kev about it, and we agreed. The camp was for the whole family. The camp was at Vision Valley in Sydney, and we would go there by train from Melbourne. I didn't know what to expect. At the train station, in Melbourne, I wondered if what I was doing was the right thing. It came so quickly. We were on the train, and it was too late to change my mind. I started to question myself, "Did I want to subject my little girl to this?"

When she came home from hospital, relatives and friends wanted me to undress her so that they could see her burns. I told them that she is no freak and she is not on show. I was worried this was going to be the same. I think that there were about 20 people from Victoria that KIDS Foundation sponsored to go on this camp. On the train, we met some really lovely people, Susie O'Neill and Dr. Sally Feelgood. We also met other families. Phillipa Field and I got along well. One of her children had been burnt as well. Another woman I met was Janet Cheetham. Her son, Andrew, had been badly burnt. After seeing Andrew, I thought to myself that Amanda was not so bad, as Andrew was in a wheelchair and was burnt from head to toe. Andrew told me that he felt really sorry for Amanda. I asked him why, because his burns were more severe than Amanda's. Andrew's response was that his treatment was finished and that Amanda had more treatment to come. Andrew was a real inspiration. Once we arrived, I realised that there were people worse off than we were. I was glad that I did go on the camp as it really helped me to understand a lot. And it was good to be able to talk to people that knew what we had been through and understood where we were coming from. I love going on these camps now; we get to catch up with everyone and see how they were getting on.

Camp Phoenix 1999 was at Mount Eliza. We met up with old friends and made some new ones. Andrew really inspired me when I saw him because he was out of his wheelchair. He had his driver's licence and his own car and was writing articles for newspapers. Andrew showed us that life does go on. Janet and I were the camp clowns as we were the only two who had fallen out of the canoe. Still, we enjoyed ourselves. We also had a blast on the giant swing and the flying fox. Archery was also a laugh as I kept missing the target. Andrew has been a great inspiration to Amanda. She was now able to see that there was hope for her. It made Amanda realise that no matter how bad your scars are, you can still do and become what you want.

My two boys also enjoy going to these camps because it helps them to understand what is going on and that there are other kids on camp they can talk to who understand. When you have a child that has been injured so badly, others in the family miss out and don't get the attention they deserve. As much as you try not to let it affect them, the ongoing treatment takes you away from them. Amanda still has to have more skin grafts for many years to come. Going to the camps has helped me to understand that bad things can happen, but there are good people out there that can help. The KIDS Foundation has been a lifeline for us. Camp Phoenix is a place for people to talk to one another who are going through the same thing. Going on these camps has helped Amanda to deal with her scars. The scars are not bothering her as much anymore, well they did, but she has learned to deal with them, and they don't slow her down.

Seeing all the other people on these camps and listening to their terrifying stories was a real learning experience for me and Kev. The emotional healing that happens at the camps just by talking to others is life changing. Being amongst like-minded people reassures me that Amanda is still my little girl and nothing has changed. She is still a beautiful little girl. Parents also get the chance to share ideas on treatments and care. I have learned to care for Amanda's burns with ease and pride. When Amanda was burnt, I was at a loss. I didn't know what the best way was to do simple things like putting on pressure garments. The treatments parents are required to do are so painful and stressful. The most valuable lesson my husband learned through these camps was how I was feeling and what Amanda's going through. This has made a big difference to our relationship, and he has been able to feel more valuable and help.

When Amanda was first burnt, Kev wouldn't put moisturiser on her and thought that he couldn't touch her without hurting her. The support staff at the KIDS Foundation helped him to better understand things. Kev was quietly suffering too. Camp Phoenix has helped Kevin to express his feelings. Amanda looks forward to going to the camps every year to catch up with people she has made friends with, especially Susie O'Neill and Dr. Sally Feelgood. Amanda adores them both. I can't say enough about the KIDS Foundation and the camp. They mean a lot to my family. I don't know how I would have coped without them. We are part of one big KIDS family when we are together; everyone is there for the same reason and on the same level. Here Amanda feels she is no different, included, and treated like a normal child.

I would like to thank Susie O'Neill and give a shout out to Dr. Sally Feelgood and Channel 10 for their support of these camps. Without them and all the other sponsors, there wouldn't be any camps. So, from a very grateful parent, a big THANK YOU for making the KIDS Foundation's Burn Survivors' Network and Camp Phoenix possible.

Dr. Feelgood, Amanda and Susie

Amanda

Taneille. Amanda and Susie

The train trip took around 12 hours, and it allowed us to really get to know the families that had joined us. We left the train and headed to the complex at Vision Valley. We were all feeling a little anxious walking into the hall, not knowing what to expect. The retreat was for families, but there were lots of little people badly injured—it was heartbreaking. The experience was quite confronting however, we met some really beautiful people that were to become part of the KIDS Foundation family.

Recently KIDS Foundation had a stand at an Officeworks Back to School Promotion. In walks Amanda with her husband and two children. It was so lovely to see her and the devotion she had for her family. They named their daughter Taneille, inspired by Teneille that has worked with the KIDS Foundation on and off for more than 16 years. In 2005, Teneille began her unrelenting persistent attempts to gain a job at the KIDS Foundation. She and my son had a part-time job together working in a clothing store my brother-in-law owned in Ballarat when her job searching began. A day wouldn't go past without Ben coming home asking if there were any jobs going at KIDS. In the end, I arranged an interview, despite the fact there were no positions, to tactfully tell her so. At the end of the interview, I had employed her. She had made such an impression that I had to find something for her to do.

Teneille is one of those bubbly, happy people that makes everyone feel good. We needed her in the Foundation to lift some spirits, and she did just that. Teneille is married to Phil and has two adorable children, Freddie and Florence. Teneille is the KIDS boomerang, returning to us from wherever life takes her. Today she continues to work from our Noosa office. Together we make a great team, creating all the visuals and the look of KIDS. Teneille remains one our longest serving loyal employees, along with Carlee Grant.

We don't meet people
by accident.
They're meant to cross
our path for a reason.

- KATHRYN PEREZ

Donna

If dealing with the psychological aftereffects of this torturous crime wasn't enough, she had a bigger battle waiting for her.

At the Vision Valley retreat in 1998. I walked into the bathroom. Sitting in a wheelchair was a lady with most of her body tightly bound in a pressure garment. It was Donna. If there was ever a person to capture the words "trust, loyalty, and kindness," Donna Carson would be the one. She is one of the most inspiring women that I have met. Her story is horrific. She was fundamental in shaping the Burn Survivors' Network and is living proof of "with the right mindset, you can overcome whatever life throws you." She says, "We were destined to meet." So true!

Donna Carson was one of those kids who couldn't wait to get to school. That never changed, except she became the teacher who couldn't wait to get to school. She was an admired school teacher in Dubbo, a country town in western NSW. In April 1994, Donna's career was cut short due to an act of violence that left her with burns to 65% of her body and a slim chance of survival. In a jealous rage, her de facto partner bashed her, doused her in petrol, and set her alight in front of her two young sons, Coe and Bodean who were 12 and 2 years old at the time. Coe yelled to his mum to "drop and roll, roll mum, roll."

Donna and Bodean

Donna spent the next six months in hospital drifting in and out of consciousness. Donna's parents were instructed to prepare funeral arrangements as they would never be taking her home alive. From that moment, Donna became known to those around her as the woman who refused to die "just because the odds said so." It was her two young sons, Coe and Bodean, that kept her fighting for her life. If dealing with the psychological aftereffects of this torturous crime wasn't enough, she had a bigger battle waiting for her. While lying in the hospital, social services stepped in and took her boys away from her and her extended family, blaming Donna for the violence. In the midst of enduring 15 months of agonising rehab, she battled her next two fights. First, to reclaim custody of her children, and second, to push for the right to take the stand at her attacker's sentencing.

When I was informed of the acceptance of a lesser plea for a guilty verdict and that the offender would walk free on parole, then to learn I was not welcomed to take the stand, to not be seen or heard, I went to the media. A journalist at the Daily Telegraph spent hours with me and even came to court. I was finally seen by the judge, and he sent the offender to jail for the week while he thought about the sentencing and the shit storm that was going down that he was not aware of at the time. Meanwhile journalist Sandra Lee from the Daily Telegraph wrote an article. I was swamped by TV presenters including Ray Martin and Helen Wellings. I decided to go with Helen Wellings from Today Tonight. They sent a film crew to Wingham and spent the next two days here filming. We got to know each other well, and they fell in love with my boys. In return for the gory details, that I know sells the show, I was allowed to put forward my angle on the show - Domestic Violence, the silent crime.

I was back in hospital when it went to air. The hospital was swamped with calls. Someone even wanted to donate their skin to me, God bless them, it doesn't quite work that way. Channel 7 had huge ratings. It was a hit. Then back at court for sentencing. There was a media frenzy waiting on the court steps. The film crew and presenter were there to protect me. Channel 7 asked me to do a follow up story with them as a favour. I agreed, as I thought the next angle could be about Victims of Crime being invisible, and victims being the most affected by crime, yet they are not involved in the procedures (as a victim of crime you report the crime and then are kept in the dark, and the sentence does not fit the crime). So, we did a second story together, and it was again good. We had good ratings and the public were talking about it, a topic of conversation. Channel 7 received many enquiries, mail, gifts, and messages, and they were all forwarded to me.

Shortly after, I was back in hospital again and came across information about a burns support group. The address was the Westmead Children's Hospital, which was just next door. So, I put on my dressing gown, walked across the road, and into the Children's Hospital. There I met a lady named Cheri who told me all the about the camps they run, but they didn't involve adult survivors. I asked if I could attend the next camp and invite some other adult survivors as well. I found her rather strange and cold, but I persisted as I thought it was a great idea. Eventually she agreed, so I asked for some posters and brochures and headed back to the hospital. By this time, I got to know quite a few adult survivors. Each time I went back in for another operation, the staff would ask me to pop into the burns unit and visit some of the patients. I visited survivors in hospital, in rehab, and sometimes in their own homes. I wrote to and sent brochures containing information on the camps to all hospitals and burns units in Sydney, leaving them in waiting rooms after I had been given permission to do so.

I had heard the funding for these camps was running very low, and it could be the last camp. This time I contacted Channel 7 and asked if they would do a favour for me, to run a third story. The story would be based on a recap of the previous two stories, my recovery, and to find financial support for the camps. That is when Susie happened to watch the current affair program, and the rest is history. We were destined to meet!

The extent of Donna's remarkable tale of survival is captured in her autobiography Judas Kisses with Debbie Richie. It traces her astonishing journey. It discovers the true emotive story of what happens when a victim turns survivor. Donna demanded to be seen and heard, and "When you've been on fire, you don't take no for an answer."

I was honoured to be part of her nomination for the NSW "Local Hero" 2004, which she won. One day, Donna rang to invite me to accompany her to Canberra to attend the Australia Day Council's Australian of the Year Awards 2004. She was deservedly recognised for her work as an advocate for burn survivors, domestic violence survivors, and victims of crime. Donna worked in three areas of Victims of Crime/Legal Systems and achieved practical changes such as court support and safety waiting rooms at courthouses. We were that excited to be meeting the Prime Minister at the time, The Hon. John Howard, and mix with Australian VIPs and celebrities.

Donna Carson with The Hon. John Howard

Bodean's highlight was getting to meet Guy Sebastian, winner of the first Australian Idol in 2003 who was performing at the open-air concert that night. Donna was shielding the secret that she was about to receive the Nations "Local Hero" 2004 Australia Day award.

Guy Sebastian, Susie and Bodean

Watching her standing at the podium addressing the thousands of Australians who had gathered on the lawns of Parliament House was the proudest moment. Donna delivered an empowering speech that captured everyone's attention through her fatigued voice that remains damaged from that horrific day that changed her life. Donna is now part of the "Australia Day Family." Every year she is invited back to Canberra to attend the Governor General's function for finalists and Prime Minister award ceremonies for Australia Day.

Donna is a true crusader, passionate educator, and an inspiring mentor for countless survivors of burns, domestic violence, and crime. She has committed her "second life" to providing support to those who are forced to endure the journey from victim to survivor. Each year we would arrive at Camp Phoenix greeted by countless new faces and families with unimaginable stories of survival. Donna would be the first person to pull the team together, and with her knowledge and firsthand experience, set about devising a plan to bringing each new survivor to a place of hope. She would quickly gain their trust and loyalty through her acts of kindness and visually obvious unique qualifications.

Donna has been awarded numerous accolades including a torchbearer of the Athens Olympic Flame in Sydney 2004 and was listed on the Who's Who in Australia. Who's Who in Australia lists persons who have contributed to Australian life on a National and International level, "I'm right up there with the men," said Donna proudly. Donna was also included in the first edition of Who's Who of Australian Women in 2006. Donna had her portrait painted by a brilliant Southern Highland artist, Dave Thomas, and entered in the 2010 and 2012 Archibald Prize competitions. Donna shares her story...

On Good Friday, April 1, 1994, my jealous and obsessive partner Garry threw petrol in my face and down my front and ignited me. My precious boys witnessed this unbelievable horror. They were 12 and 2 years old. I suffered full thickness burns to 65% of my body, my entire face, neck, chest, shoulders, arms, hands, all my fingers, my legs, and my feet. I have extensive and permanent damage to my throat, airway, and lungs, and I was not expected to survive. I spent five and a half agonizing months in Sydney's Westmead Burns Unit, followed by 15 months of rehab. But I survived.

As a burn's patient, life became pure darkness and thick, choking blackness. The horrendous pain, the anguish, the unimaginable agony is beyond words or comprehension. I truly ache when imagining what a child must think while enduring burns.

At the time, my parents were advised to prepare for my funeral, and Social Services were concocting an unimaginable story that Garry and I had participated in a suicide pact. This allegation was done without any investigation, nor following their procedures and without involving the police. They took Coe and Bodean away from my extended family that were caring for them. Even years later, they still hadn't apologised, so I took them to the courts. Meanwhile, the police did investigate, took statements, and determined that I was a victim of crime. The case had been held up because the police were told I would die, and they were waiting to be able to charge the offender with murder. I became the women that refused to die.

My friend, Gabby, an English nurse who was also doused in petrol and burnt by her ex in 1996, has been a constant support in my life. We have commonalities in our unthinkable circumstances and with having to deal with our ex-partners getting out of jail.

As a burn survivor, I would write and visit hospitals and homes providing support, hope, and friendship. I was often contacted by others who have read Judas Kisses and needed to talk or who were looking for information concerning domestic violence, court procedures, or victim's rights. I have journeyed with many on their road to recovery - being their cheer squad, comedy relief, sharing in their sadness, and celebrating in their achievements. I remember how good it felt to receive mail while in hospital, and my reward is the satisfaction of them knowing that they are not alone or forgotten. An important piece of knowledge that I have passed on to them is about the KIDS Foundation and the Burn Survivors' Network. I would tell them about the Burns Camps, where the families can get together for a few days to share their stories and just relax and have fun. They are gatherings of ordinary people from all walks of life - different cultures, religions, and ages - who have survived an extraordinary ordeal.

We decided to do things a little differently the following year at the NSW retreat. It worked in well to tie my trip to the retreat in with corporate meetings in Sydney. After the meetings, I hired a car and headed to the Blue Mountains where the retreat was being held. Two nurses from the Alfred and an occupational therapist from Caulfield Rehab Centre, along with Andy, decided to drive from Melbourne and were going to arrive around dinner time. Arriving just before dinner, I settled into our hut I was to share with the Melbourne crew, then headed to the dining room. I remember walking into a room with families seated at tables. I sat down, and opposite me was a gentleman with one eye who literally had one side of his face melted off. He had a small hole where his mouth was, and was temporarily surviving by taking in nourishment via a straw. Another gentleman at the table was in a wheelchair with half his leg missing after it was "gravel-rashed" off in a motorbike accident. There were young children in pressure garments from head to toe, with their innocent eyes peering through the eye openings. The only thing I could stomach was a small bowl of jelly. I politely left, got into the hire car, drove to a small town, sat in the car, and cried, "What was I getting myself into?" Then I got a call from the Melbourne crew to say, "We are all okay, but we have been in a car accident." I can't remember how they got there, but they arrived in the early hours of the next morning. That night I did a lot of soul searching and in the end told myself to pull it together. Despite their changed appearance, look into their eyes. That is the advice I now give to new volunteers that find the camps quite confronting.

One day, one of the young boys rang me and said he wasn't really keen to go on another retreat as for him it was too focused on medical-based therapies and psychology. He said, "I get my therapy through sharing experiences with others that have similar stories to tell." Quite a few others felt the same way. That is when a group of mums suggested we set up the Burn Survivors' Network that catered for children and families Australia wide.

Fran and Donna

Fran (Giselle's mum) and Donna were real troopers and did a lot of the groundwork helping to establish the program and supporting new families. What survivors wanted was to see that they had hope and what their "new normal life" would look like. They gained this from the courageous and inspirational people they met through the program and camps. There was always someone worse off than they were.

Giselle, Fran and Kate

I wanted to say something
to make her pain go away
and make everything better.
But, I realised that
there was no answer.
Bad things happen to good people.
Rain always falls on the
people who deserve
nothing less than the sun.

- MACKENZIE HERBERT

How that morning changed our lives as a family unit.

Fran was instrumental in establishing the Burns Survivors Network. She is the Mum of Giselle, a beautiful little 18-month-old at the time of the traumatic event. This was her experience as a mother of a child who was scalded and how it has changed their lives as a family unit.

Please realise, no matter how small or large your burn is, the one thing we have in common is our lives changed forever. There is no experience more distressing for a parent than seeing her child scalded or burnt. Prevention is everything!

July 12, 1994, on a cold, wet, miserable afternoon at about 3:20 p.m. School had finished and the kids were home from school, Monique age 6, Vincent age 4, and Giselle age 18 months old. A girlfriend had popped in for a cup of coffee. We were talking in the kitchen while waiting for the kettle to boil. As most toddlers, Giselle was wondering around the kitchen, and the other children were watching TV. Our two cups were already on the kitchen bench. The kettle clicks! I walked over and poured the water into the cups; I turned and asked Sue is she would like sugar. No sooner had I finished that Giselle was on her toes feeling the bench. My reaction to what I was going to witness was horror; my hands could not grab her fast enough. I heard the scream of pain like I had never heard before. The cup had over balanced onto the saucer and the hot liquid ran down her face and ear. Her face and ears began to swell. In a matter of seconds, her skin could not hold the fluid, and it started to split like a plastic bag melting with heat.

I jumped into the shower fully clothed. As I started to undress Giselle, I soon learned the damage was not only to her face, but also to her arm, neck, and chest. I kept reminding myself to stay calm as my two other children watched in shock. My daughter Monique was yelling at me, "What have you done to her!" and the tears rolled down her face uncontrollably. My girlfriend Sue called for an ambulance and within minutes they arrived, and we were transported to Ryde Hospital. If I had been more educated in burns, I would have realised I should have kept her under the shower for at least 20 minutes. I could have prevented Giselle's burns from becoming full thickness. I was not to know that this would be the last time I would return home for six weeks. On examination, I was advised the hospital did not have a burns ward. They decided that they would organise for Giselle to be cleaned up and that we would return for daily dressings. The doctor said, "It shouldn't even leave a scar." I looked at him in a state of shock and asked him if he was serious. I told the doctor that I was not prepared to take Giselle home in this condition. My husband had just arrived at the end of the conversation. I caught his eyes as he looked at Giselle. I saw his whole world just crumble in front of him. I was a mess, confused, I just wanted Giselle to stop crying, she was in pain and terribly frightened. They gave her an injection for pain relief, and she sat on my husband's lap drifting off to sleep. I had to get my child out of this hospital. I decided to phone 000 and got an ambulance to take Giselle to the Children's Hospital. They asked for an address for pick up. They questioned the fact that I was already in a hospital. They explained that other accidents would get first priority for pick up. We could have driven Giselle to the Children's Hospital ourselves; the only problem was that we could not put a seat belt on her because of the burns to her chest.

At 10:45 p.m., seven hours later, we arrived at the Children's Hospital. They were expecting us because they had heard I was a neurotic mother and that I was over-protective. To be honest, at that point, I knew I was doing the best I could for my child, and I didn't care what anyone thought. On examination, I was told Giselle would be admitted to the burns ward and we would have to stay for at least 12 days to have daily baths to keep the infection away and to scrub back the dead skin. I told them I was confused as the other hospital said, "She would not even scar!" They continued to tell me that Giselle would probably require skin grafts, but this would not happen until after 12 days. We were taken over to the burns ward. I was still wet from the shower, and I asked my husband to go home and organise the children, to pack a bag for me and one for the children to go to grandmas. Giselle and I sat in a semi dark room, and the only thing of comfort was her dummy to console her. I couldn't bear the thought of back tracking the events of that afternoon. It was unimaginable pain. What were my husband, family, and friends going to think of me?

A nurse disturbed my thoughts. "Fran," she whispered. "We are going to give Giselle a bath and get her pressure bandages on. It will help prepare Giselle for the upcoming days." I thought this was odd. A bath at midnight? Giselle held onto me. There was no way we were going to be separated. The first stage of my nightmare became real as they submerged her into the bath. Giselle screamed uncontrollably, and I almost collapsed to the floor. How could I possibly watch this happen to her for 12 days? It was too painful. The bath was too unbearable to watch or to even discuss. The nurse asked if I would prefer to wait outside, and I said that there was no way that I was going to leave her side until we went home. Giselle was wrapped in bandages, somewhat like a mummy, white bandages covered her head and upper body, and she also wore a neck brace. They gave me a cot for Giselle, but there was no way of putting her into it. My lap became her bed as we sat in the chair for what was left of the night.

Morning arrived and so did my husband, parents, and children. Mum's face said it all. This was torture for them to see a grandchild in so much pain. We had never experienced anyone being burnt before; I was not prepared. Vincent came over for a kiss and a cuddle, but Monique kept her distance. I begged her to give me a kiss, but she kept on ignoring me until she let it out. "I hate you. Look at what you have done to Giselle!" I was hurting so bad, I felt I had to keep it together or my family would fall apart. There were so many emotions, and we were all hurting. Each individual in his or her own silence. A councillor came by and introduced herself. She asked if Paul and I had a moment she would like to talk to us. I had no energy to talk to her. I had no idea what I should be feeling; my whole world was caving in. We were told that Giselle would need a feed tube, as the amount of milk she was taking through her bottle was nowhere near the level of calcium that she was going to require. In the morning as we approached the door for a bath, Giselle started to pull away from the door screaming. I couldn't believe the memory of the bath, the evening before, had scared Giselle so badly. The nurses organised medication for the following days. She was given it 10 minutes before the bath, and it lasted for about 45 minutes. Excuse the expression, but she was "off her face." There is no other way to describe it. It was to relax her and enable her to forget. I thought to myself, I might need a couple of bottles myself just to forget this nightmare.

Giselle's personality slowly started to fade. She no longer spoke, and she went back to crawling. She had regressed approximately eight months in age. Friends and family organised a roster. Someone would always be there for support and a shoulder to lean on. There were eight beds in our ward, four beds occupied by toddlers in the same condition as Giselle. I couldn't believe that this burn injury by coffee was quite common. I was truly alarmed! The days dragged on, dates and days were irrelevant, and baths were the main priority. My other children were shuffled from friend's houses during the week and grandmas on the weekend. During their visits, they would often cry when it was time to go home, as they wanted me to return home with them. It became quite obvious; their lives, too, were dramatically changed.

By this time, the strain on the family was taking its toll. We didn't realise the skin graft would have to come from Giselle's legs, and now we were troubled with the fact that her perfect legs would also become scarred. People were now trying to make us feel better by saying, "Don't worry, you can grow Giselle's hair and you won't even see the scars. Choose the right clothes and no one will ever know." We soon realised that we had to encourage Giselle to be herself. No one should dictate what she should wear or how she wore her hair. Why should we hide her burns for the comfort of others? We had to come together as a family and support each other no matter what.

After her grafts, Giselle became stronger by the day. Three weeks later, we were allowed home. The hospital had become our home. The security of the hospital walls and staff was comforting as we all had something in common, no one to judge us or make us feel different. We were burn survivors.

Our family life became very busy. We were all involved at bath times and rubbing Shoreline cream over Giselle's body three times a day to keep her grafts moist. Not to mention putting on Giselle's pressure garments, we had a headpiece, tee shirt, and neck brace. This was worn 24 hours for 18 months. Monique and Vincent were excited I was back home and that I could drop them off at school. The excitement was soon overwhelming when the children noticed things to be very different; people were staring at their sister. I gave them a cuddle and told them things would be okay and that I would see them in the afternoon. I decided the sooner things got back to normal, the better for all of us.

I went to our local shopping centre to do a food shop. The curiosity on peoples' faces as they wondered what had happened to this child. While I was waiting in the queue to pay for my groceries, a lady behind me was watching Giselle sitting in the trolley. She turned to me and asked, "What happened to your little girl?" I answered, "She pulled a cup of coffee over herself." The lady looked for a moment and then replied, "Well, you're a stupid mother, you won't let that happen again." I was mortified, and my eyes filled with tears as I grabbed Giselle out of the trolley and ran for the car. I was not prepared for this latest experience. Yes, you may have guessed it. I was a mess, and the tears flooded my face with the guilt of what had happened to my daughter. On arriving home, I raced in the door and phoned the social worker at the hospital and just let out all of my emotions. I couldn't believe that this experience had confirmed our lives would be changed forever. I realised my family would need major help if we were going to get through it.

October 1994, three months after Giselle's accident, we were invited to a family burns camp. My husband and I thought it might be a waste of time as Giselle was only 18 months old. What could she possibly get out of it? Well … I was wrong! It was the beginning of a new way of life for us. One weekend with other families in the same situation, time of no judgement, the children could have fun with the support of other family members who had been through similar experiences. My family had come back to life; we learned how to survive the difficult times. We shared our fears and concerns, and the healing had begun. I believe these family burns camps are beneficial in the healing processes not only for the burn survivor but also for the whole family. They offer emotional support, comfort, encouragement, and reassurance. It teaches our children that they can trust in others and that others can listen to their concerns without judgement. We learn that we all have different needs but at the end of the day we are all survivors.

I know that Giselle is on a learning journey. She will have to deal with many different phases through her life, but if we can keep on giving support for these camps to keep going on, then I know that there will be great appreciation from all our families. We can make a true difference in the lives of burn survivors. As the years move on and the camps come and go, the true identities of these young men and women begin to surface. I have met some wonderful people through these camps, and I am proud to say they are my friends. At one camp, I noticed our new family members had so much frustration and pain, as they struggled to come to terms with the tragedy that had come to their lives. For these families, it was the first time they had come into contact with other burn survivors and their families. The most rewarding part came when these families started to exchange stories and really listened to each other. The hope and the healing process began to shine through. There is no reason to go through the pain alone. There are so many people that want to help. The best advice I could give anyone in the same situation is to get in contact with other families and share your experiences. It helps to know that other families have either been there or are going through your same hurt and anger. Remember there is always a light at the end of the tunnel! It's amazing how one decision can change your life forever.

Giselle

Jess, Giselle and Brittney

Giselle's reflection...

For me, I'm thankful that I don't remember the accident. I was only 18 months old when my mum was enjoying having a friend over for afternoon tea. Without mum realising, I reached up onto the kitchen bench and knocked over the cup. The hot coffee spilled all over the side of my face, neck, and chest area. It also splashed over my arms. Mum captures the story, but even though I don't remember the time spent in hospital or the pain I went through, I do have my childhood photos wearing pressure bandages and suits to help my skin heal and stretch as I grew with my skin grafts. Who would have thought coffee could do so much damage?

While I was very young, mum and my family protected me from other people's hurtful comments they made about me. They would stick up for me when I was too little to comprehend the words and actions of others. As I grew older, and I became aware of the hurtful words of others, I realised the benefit of attending the Burns Camps. I will never forget one of the many times that I was bullied for my scars. I was in year six when a boy came up to me at lunch time and decided to make jokes about my scars. This then implanted in my mind that I was different from the other children. What do people think about me? Should I feel ashamed and embarrassed about my scars?

Going to high school is always daunting for any teenager. I was not only nervous, but I was afraid of attending swimming carnivals where it was compulsory to attend. I would be faced with people looking at my scars. When going out to the shops or to the movies with my friends, I used to always cover my chest with my hand because I

Giselle on her wedding day

was embarrassed and self-conscious. I was so worried people would stare at my scars. In 2019, my dreams came true when I was married, and I am now 28 years old. Growing up, I always wanted a princess wedding with the big white dress, flowers everywhere, and to celebrate with my amazing family and friends. I was lucky enough to get an amazing designer to design and create my magical dress. When starting the design, my first thought that came to my mind was, "Should I cover my scars?" I wondered what my wedding dress would look like if my scars were showing. These thoughts are always going to be with me. I chose to wear a low V neckline dress, which would show my scars, and I am so proud I did it as I absolutely loved my wedding dress. I remind myself during these times that everyone is different, everyone is beautiful in their own way, and I am strong because I have gone through this.

From 18 months until I was 17 years old, I attended the Burn Survivors' Camps. This became a part of my life. We were lucky enough to attend the annual camp plus other benefits throughout the year. Once a year, we would travel to the chosen destination for that year. This was something that I would look forward to and count down the days until the next time we would go again. I met some amazing people whom I could connect with. We all had different stories, different up bringing, and different family culture, but we all could relate to one another. The burns camp isn't just for the burns survivor, it's for their family as well. Some people don't realise that it impacts the people around you as well. They see and feel the struggle, the pain, and the journey that their family member is going through or has gone through. The camps were a little get away to forget about our insecurities and just have fun with one another. I remember doing different activities that took me out of my comfort zone, creating life-long friends who lived in other states so the only time we saw each other was at the camps, meeting celebrities, and having themed dress up nights. I had the honour of attending balls and special events where I was able to fundraise money for Burns Camps.

I will always be forever grateful to Susie O'Neill and the burn survivor family. Susie always made us feel special, she gave us hope and strength in the difficult times, but she also took interest and shared our goals and achievements. Susie changed my childhood and life for the better, and I am so grateful she made a difference to my life.

In 2020 our SeeMore Safety program went to 10,000 kindergartens/preschools, with 400,000 take home books printed and included in the packs for children and their families. At the request of educators an additional 60,000 books were printed. The preschool where Giselle teaches was one to receive the pack and books. Our paths cross again in a different way... In February 2021 I received a text message from Giselle that read:

> *Hi Susie how are you?*
>
> *I thought I'd share with you that I walked into my classroom at work the other day and noticed your "SeeMore bug safety the tiny germs we can see" book on the shelf.*
>
> *I was so excited and couldn't wait to read it with the children. They absolutely loved it and were so engaged. I then did a germs experiment after reading the book.*
>
> *I was telling my Director how I know you and she was so happy and asked whether you'd come in to chat with the children. I told her you lived in Melbourne.*
>
> *Does SeeMore do zoom visits with preschool age children?*
>
> *xx Giselle*

We can't wait to take SeeMore to visit the children at Giselle's preschool soon.

Nellie, Patrick, Lachie and Darcy

Without music,
life would be a mistake.

- FRIEDRICH NIETZSCHE

Jai

"You got it wrong Jai, you aren't a part of the community. You're part of our family now."

Jai, now a talented musician, had been experiencing severe sinus problems, so he covered his head with a towel over a bowl of steaming water with eucalyptus oil. In a split second, the water went from the bowl onto Jai's chest and lap. The result was five weeks in the Women's and Children's Hospital in Adelaide. Third degree burns to both inner and outer thighs and second degree to his chest and hand. He had skin grafts to all the third degree burns on both his thighs. Over the past 10 years, he has had over 30 day-surgeries to treat the resulting scars. Jai's account of his accident...

At the age of eight, I experienced a serious burn injury. I was scalded with hot water and suffered burns from my mid chest to mid thighs. I am still having regular day-surgeries to manage the scarring.

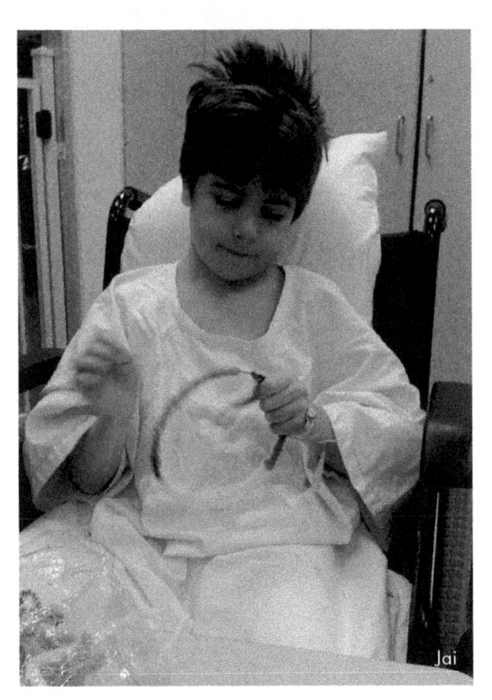

Jai

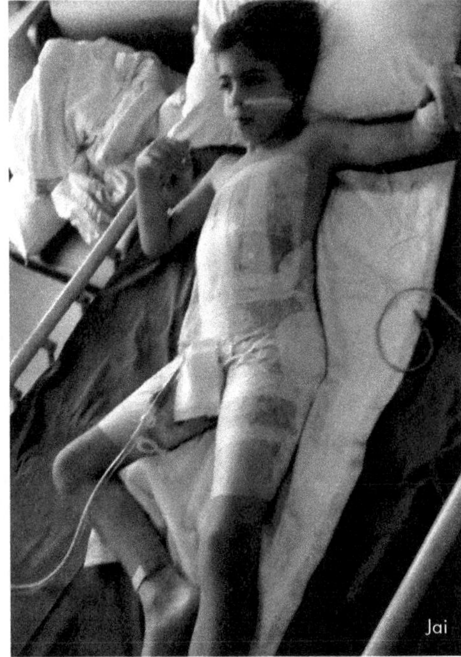

Jai

If I was to sum up in two words what being part of the KIDS family means it would be life-changing. This comes both from the perspective of a burns survivor and as someone who helps the kids at the camp. This is an account of my very first camp.

Beautiful, gorgeous, stunning. No one word can describe the experience that was Camp Phoenix. When we arrived at the ferry departure zone, we were instantly drawn towards a sea of yellow shirts, the KIDS Foundation. Once we'd ported at Moreton Bay Island, we were greeted and introduced to the staff before we went for a meeting. Inside of the "Kallatina" meeting room was KIDS Foundation space, and it became very clear very soon that this was a well and properly run organisation. They introduced us all, gave us each a "Big Buddy," and then we had lunch while talking and learning about each other.

Chris and Jai

Most of the participants were just greeting old friends, not having the trouble of making new ones, so they looked very comfortable. Those who were new (like me, I'm sure) looked obviously out of place and uncomfortable. I noticed that by having their appointed new buddies, the kids felt like they had a way into this community and quickly became acquainted with other children of the same age category. My mum suggested that I went out to grab a drink with this guy called Tom, and I was hesitant, but went along with it. In that very moment, I had my way into the community, and Tom and I have become great mates since. After Tom, it was easy to get to know others over lunches and dinners that were shared. Everyday there was a schedule of activities, free time, food breaks, and group activities that seemed dauntingly strict at first, but in reality were very flexible, and the staff were great at adjusting the schedule to fit everyone's needs and wants. We got to Tangalooma in time for a late lunch. The food was fabulous, and afterwards I learned that this was the first camp that the food was cooked by the volunteers of the KIDS Foundation. Six people did a fantastic job of cooking for the whole camp's lunches and dinners. Breakfast was also covered in the first day by the volunteers coming around to every room and dropping off these breakfast bags with all the food we'd require to make breakfast for the next three days.

Free time was a useful time for me to get to know everyone when we were down at the pool. At dinner time, I went to Tom's room and talked with him long into the night before reluctantly returning to my room upstairs. By the end of the first day, I already knew about half of everyone's names, Anna, Brock, Rhys, Christian, Tom, and more. The next few days were just as good as the first, with different meals and activities every day. We had our first group activity on the second day. It was an interesting session about mindfulness and how to be mindful in our daily lives.

The last day was one of the saddest and happiest days of my life. We started off by doing some fun activities such as quad-biking and preparing for the disco that night. The day passed quickly, and then we entered the hall dressed up and ready to disco, but before we partied there were some other matters to go over first. The PHOENIX awards were first, and each letter of the word "phoenix" represents a different award. I do not remember all of them, but I do remember the name of the one that I had won, and that was the "New Kid on the Block" award. This award is a great way for the newcomers to be recognised, and I won a nice pair of VR goggles. After the awards ceremony, there was this thing called "The Panel," and that is an array of seats set up giving anybody who wants to the opportunity to talk. The volunteers who sit in those seats then can talk about how they got burnt or just any important story in general. Tom suggested that I go up and talk about my story and why I was there, so I did.

During my speech, I thanked the group for letting me into their community so quickly, and afterwards a woman named Leanne came up to me and said, "You got it wrong Jai, you aren't a part of the community. You're part of our family now." That meant a lot to me and showed me just how wonderful the people at this place were. When I was flying home later on, I cried solidly for the second half of the trip. It felt like I was leaving a part of my heart there in Tangalooma. That was because throughout that weekend, I had just found another family, then I left it, and I longed to spend more time with them. Now my mum Melissa is a part of the KIDS team that organises the camps. She has arranged sponsorship to run a TANGO (Together Achieving New Goals and Opportunities) Camp in Adelaide for the next few years. I want the kids to leave here feeling that same sense of connection and longing, because then we know that we have done the right thing and made a safe, loving extension of the KIDS Foundation family here in Adelaide.

Jai

Jai and Ruby

All the darkness
in the world cannot
extinguish the light
of a single candle.

- ST. FRANCIS OF ASSISI

Adam

He no longer thinks of himself as a burn survivor, he sees it as part of who he is.

All over the world people are getting burned, not only in developed countries like Australia but in underdeveloped nations, tiny atolls, and most certainly in countries in the midst of armed struggle. It's something probably not often considered by us in the burns ward at the Alfred, and in my experience, almost never considered in the broader community. Perhaps then it is worthwhile for me to tell a little of my story; a tale of a very lucky person burned in one such place.

I boarded my flight to Indonesia at Sydney airport on the afternoon of September 17, 1999. I briefly noticed a sign advertising travel insurance and felt cause for a small, self-satisfied smile. My girlfriend had blown what I knew to be a good few months living money by SE Asian standards on insurance I figured was virtually impossible to collect on anyway. I wouldn't fall for such propaganda. When the money was running short, I'd have the extra cash to see us through (and undoubtedly some smart remark about the wisdom of the seasoned traveller).

A few months later, we found ourselves on a tiny island off the east coast of Thailand. Basically, I wanted to get my divemaster's license, and everyone we had met said this was the cheapest place to do it. Perhaps there's another moral in here about being a cheapskate. The details of small island living are not really relevant, so I will skip to the main event.

The weather had deteriorated to such a degree that, although this was a common tourist destination, no boats could come in or leave. Unable to dive, many looked for other ways to entertain themselves, and although many staples were running low, there was plenty of beer. One night, unable to make it home, I crashed on the floor of a friend's bungalow. From stories I was later told, I understand she lit a candle, and the mosquito net blew into it during the night.

I was dragged from the fire by someone staying in a bungalow nearby. Suffering severe burns to 60% of my body on an island with virtually no medical facilities, pretty well as far from the Thai mainland as I could be, with no hope of getting transport back due to the weather, you could say at this stage things weren't looking good. It seems harsh to say, but had I been a Thai native, they would have said a few mantras and buried my body. In fact, had I been a dumb white boy, without insurance and no one to help, the story would be quite similar. I want to be clear that what followed was just blind luck; a perfect alignment of the stars if you believe such things.

First, the other girl who was burned was insured to the eyeballs. Still, this did neither of us any good because there was simply no way to get transport off the island at any price. But second, a group of very eager divers had chartered a helicopter to fly them to the island that morning. The girl's insurance company agreed to foot the bill for our inclusion on the return trip, and someone up there was definitely on our side.

This got us as far as a small town called Surat Thani, chiefly known for being the jumping off point for the islands in the region. There was a small hospital there and blessed morphine but no burns facilities. My partner was frantically phoning everyone she could think of who might be able to help us. A simple thing, which, on its own, would be out of reach to the average Thai person.

Luck smiled again, and it turned out that Bangkok - of all the cities in SE Asia had a specialised burns unit. The Australian and English embassies were able to organize a light plane to take us to Bangkok, and eventually we were admitted to the Siriraj burns unit.

I hate to labour the point, but my survival was based largely on blind luck, the experience of a medical insurance company that didn't want anything to do with me, and the tenacity of my partner who was not about to watch any transport leave without us on it no matter what. This is Thailand, a developing nation, and like many developing countries, life, and labour, is cheap. Just ask any clothing company.

Money talks and bullshit walks and the average Thai person's yearly wage is far less than the monthly wage of a badly paid office worker in Australia. On the burns ward, each day they calculate the medication and dressings you are likely to need, and a family member must go to the cashier to pay for it. What you cannot pay for will not be issued, though usually a nurse will help you to decide what you can most do without. After my family bought special medication for my badly infected burns, the nurses christened me "The million Bhat boy." The disparity between what I and the Thai people on the ward could afford was quite marked - even should you desperately need the medication, there is no exception. No easy 12-month, interest free plan is offered.

But like the villagers I met in my travels, though the system that they live and work under may be harsh, the people are incredibly generous. One of the nurses would always go through the medication list with my mum and cross off anything that they already had in stock. Blood was incredibly expensive and sometimes simply impossible to get, and I needed a lot, so the head nurse made a deal with the blood bank that if people donated in my name then I could have it for free. Not only did the nurses and the doctors on the ward all donate, but they herded their boyfriends, girlfriends, and brothers and sisters down as well. After that, I could have had a complete blood changeover with some spare.

When I was at my worst, they pitched together to pay a monk to come up and bless my room. In fact, I thought my hallucinations were getting worse when he piled in wearing his orange robes, spraying the room with holy water. It seems unfair to me, perhaps because I've had more than my fair share of luck, that by the simple fact of your birth, instead of an accident summoning ambulances, rescue teams, and highly trained medical assistance, it will summon close family and a priest. I'm not saying I have the answers or that I would reject the luck of birth that saved my life, but in those quiet times when you sit back and count your blessings, don't you wish it could be like that for everybody?

I wrote the above while I was recovering in the Alfred Hospital in Melbourne. It was not too long after that I went to rehab and had to start thinking about what it would mean to go back into the community and live independently. So much had changed in my life since that fire around 18 months prior. I had scars literally everywhere, although my face had been only partial thickness burns and just in patches. Because of all the complications in Thailand and multiple organ failures, I was really starting from scratch again. I couldn't talk without a little vibrating device called a Servox that made me sound like a Dialect from Doctor Who due to damage to the inside of my throat from the prolonged time with a breathing tube. I was learning to walk, to write, and to hold a knife and fork. The long period of being bed ridden had caused my muscles to atrophy to such a degree that I couldn't even get myself out of bed without help. It took a long time in rehab to start winning back independence, and many amazing people helped me in that journey.

This was the point I was at when my occupational therapist, who was working with me on day releases and getting the apartment ready with aids for my eventual release, told me that she had been speaking to a woman called Susie O'Neill who was organising a camp for burn survivors at Sovereign Hill. Initially I was reluctant to go - I still had significant dressings that needed to be done daily, and I was walking with a frame. I was uneasy about my appearance and unsure whether anyone would even be able to understand my electronic voice. I don't think I would have gone until I found out that you could bring family members along as well. I felt like if I could bring my partner that she could support me, and even if no one else would talk to me, at least I wouldn't feel so awkward and alone.

We went, and the rest, as they say, is history. We ended up sleeping in bunk rooms. I shared with a guy who was much younger than me, but he had been burned about five years before and had very similar burns to my own. We shared stories, surgeries that had worked, and ones that hadn't. He told me his experiences and some of the things that would likely be in front of me, and we traded approaches to getting through. We became good friends and stayed in touch for many years after that first camp. Everyone on the camp was very welcoming, the other survivors, their families, and the volunteers all made me feel really welcome and part of their community.

It was hard, tiring, and emotionally draining for me as I was still weak, and to say I was out of shape would be the most extreme of understatements. But it was an uplifting experience for me and gave me hope that I might fit in again. I've been going to Camp Phoenix nearly every year since that first camp back in 2001. At first, I went because I just needed the contact and to share stories with other survivors and their families. Being a burn survivor was such a big part of my life, and there were so few people to discuss it with. Later, as my life began to go back to normal and I didn't see myself as just a burn survivor, I kept going to try and help other survivors if I could. And then when I had kids, I took them with me to camp so that they could be around other burn survivors and realise that I am not the only person with scars and that people, no matter what their injury or appearance, are just people and it is all normal. I have met some of the most amazing people on camp and many of them are part of mine and my family's lives.

Jacqui and Adam

In fact, my first date with my partner Jacqui was when I was sharing my story at a KIDS Foundation fundraising dinner at the Hyatt in Melbourne in 2002. We have been together for nearly 20 years now with two amazing kids, Lily and Jasper. She has been to every camp with me since then as well as some of the Camp TANGOs where I have been able to help mentor younger burn survivors and injured teenagers.

My life is so different now to what it was back on that first Camp Phoenix. Jacqui and I went to England so that I could get some surgery around 2003, and I can now speak without the Servox. I put myself through University and have forged a successful career in computer programming. I no longer think of myself as a burn survivor, but it is part of who I am. Jacqui and the kids have been a huge part of that process of moving on, but Camp Phoenix and the network of people I met through the KIDS Foundation have been a significant part of that too.

Adam, Jacqui, Lily, Jasper and Susie

Adam reassures others they are not alone. There is a whole KIDS village of incredible individuals that are here to support them in times of need. He is a great mentor for younger burn survivors and injured teenagers, supporting them through their recovery and most importantly giving them hope. Annie's story is a testament to the impact one survivor can have on another.

Comedy is acting out optimism.

- ROBIN WILLIAMS

Annie

You wouldn't think that being burnt as a teenager would turn you into a comedian, but for me, it made perfect sense.

When I was 16 years old, I was camping out in regional Victoria when a minor injury turned into something much worse. I was preparing dinner, peeling a pumpkin with a pocket-knife when the knife slipped. It cut the middle finger on my left hand and blood started trickling from the wound.

Myself, and the people I was camping with, struggled to locate a first aid kit. After about 20 minutes of walking around trying to find a bandage with no luck, I began feeling dizzy and panicked. Someone eventually took charge and told me to stand still, so I did. The last thing I remember was looking out into the distance and seeing the trees spinning and swaying.

I have no memory of fainting into a campfire, which is probably for the best. I've been told since that there were plenty of people around who rushed to grab me as soon as they saw what happened. Unfortunately, the coals were incredibly hot, and it only took a few seconds to cause severe burns. When I became conscious again, the first thing I smelt was burning hair. It's so distinct I'll never forget it. I could only see out of my left eye, and I couldn't speak properly because my lips were completely swollen. My friend Georgia appeared. I could tell she was trying to hold it together. The first words she said to me were, "Everything's going to be alright. You'll be gorgeous again in no time." These words were haunting because as a self-conscious teen, I didn't think I was gorgeous to begin with. I didn't know what had happened, but I knew immediately that it was seriously bad.

An adult drove us to a small rural hospital in his ute. They called ahead so a doctor and nurse could meet us there. I was told to keep squeezing Georgia's hand every few seconds to indicate I was still conscious. I squeezed incredibly hard for the whole journey. I was in shock and went overboard with the squeezing. In my mind, the fact I was feeling something meant I was alive, and it felt like I was hanging onto dear life with every squeeze.

The doctor at the rural hospital did an assessment and sent me on to the Northern Hospital in Epping for proper treatment. I was taken in an ambulance where I got to suck on the "green whistle" for pain relief. It did the job, because I remember being incredibly giddy with excitement that I was riding in an ambulance and immediately forgot all of my worries.

When I arrived, the nurses cut all of my clothes off and gave me more pain relief. The doctors stated I had 10% burns to my face and neck. The most severe was third degree (now known as full thickness) burns near my jaw. I had first degree (superficial) burns to my forehead and second degree burns all over the left side of my face and down my neck and chest.

The clothes I was wearing, luckily, didn't catch fire. The doctors also commented on how lucky I was that I was fully unconscious during the incident. I didn't have any internal burns, which could have happened if I had been breathing when I fell.

My family arrived at the hospital and my aunt took one look at me and started wailing. One of the nurses told me they had no idea I was Chinese until my family arrived. The swelling from the burns was so bad the staff couldn't even tell my ethnicity. I spent most of my time sleeping because there wasn't much else to do. I couldn't read or watch television because I still couldn't see out of my left eye. It was glued shut from the swelling, and it was a waiting game to find out if my eye had been damaged. The worst-case scenario was that I'd lost sight in that eye, and that terrified me.

I looked forward to mealtimes the most. To be honest, I don't really mind hospital food, even now. Strangely, one of my fondest memories of being in hospital was when my dad came to visit me one lunch time. He fed me orange jelly from a spoon. There wasn't much to it, but we shared a moment of peace, which was rare in my turbulent relationship with my dad. We had a big age difference of 64 years, so we butted heads on a range of issues during my teen years. I suppose it reminded me of simpler times as a kid, when my parents protected me, and my biggest worries were which flavour of jelly we should make next.

The other thing I enjoyed was going on a daily walk of the empty hospital corridors at night, accompanied by my mum or one of the nurses. It was the only time I felt I was free to roam without judgement. I had lost a lot of weight from stress. I looked in the mirror one day after a shower and felt the bones of my spine with my hand. I remember thinking I looked like a stegosaurus, and it made me chuckle.

After a week, I was taken into the theatre to have skin grafts. Doctors told me they would take skin from my bottom and put it on my left eyelid. I came out of the surgery high as a kite, thinking it had all been done and there was a patch of skin missing from my butt. A day later, I was told they didn't need to do the surgery after all because the surgeons decided my eyelid would heal on its own. They washed the dirt and dust out of my hair and gave my skin a scrub instead. My butt remains intact to this day.

Thankfully, my eyesight had survived the accident, and I was able to see properly out of both eyes again. I started watching "Scrubs," an American comedy series set in a hospital. The show made hospitals less scary, and I laughed my way through the rest of my time there.

That experience planted the seed for my future comedy career. I could see the value of comedy as a form of therapy and as a coping mechanism.

When I left the hospital, I spent about three months recovering at home. In the months after the accident, I experienced two states of mind. On one hand, I didn't want to live any more. Every day I woke up, with a compression mask on and silicon sheets stuck to my face, and remembered what had happened to me. I wished so badly that I could wake up in a different body that hadn't been burnt. Whenever I went out, people would stare at me and ask me what happened to my face, like I owed them an answer. I was depressed for a long time. On the other hand, I was grateful to be alive. There were still so many things I wanted to do, and I realised your life could change, or be taken away, in an instant.

I started borrowing stand-up DVDs from my local video store to pass the time and to cheer me up. Before I knew it, I'd cleaned out the store and watched everything they had. Before my accident, I had thought about trying stand-up, as a bucket list item, but suddenly I felt like the dream couldn't wait any longer. Even though performing comedy scared me, it paled in comparison to how scared I was of death and of living an unfulfilled life.

I saw an advertisement for the Melbourne International Comedy Festival's Class Clowns Competition. Each year, they search for "Australia's Funniest Teenager." I was doing drama classes outside of school and had a bit of performing experience, so I entered.

A woman named George McEnroe hosted my first ever gig at the Malthouse Theatre in Melbourne. She's a total boss who went on to create "Sheeba," Australia's leading all-women rideshare service. During that gig, I still had bandages on my face, but I didn't talk about what happened to me because it was still too fresh. Instead, I had material about being a Chinese kid, about my friends and family, and embarrassing stories.

I made it through to the Victorian State final and then through to the National Final. Less than a year after my burns, I found myself performing at the main stage of the Melbourne Town Hall, which has a capacity of 2,000 people. They had professional comedians warming up the crowd that day. One of them was musician and comedian Sammy J. I now work with him on ABC Radio Melbourne as one of his regular guests on the breakfast show.

In 2016, I googled "burns charities in Australia" and came across the KIDS Foundation. I initially thought I could get involved with a charity as a mentor, but I had no idea how much it would help with my own healing.

I went to my first camp that year, by myself. The next year I brought my sister, Anna. (Yes, we have almost identical names, and it has certainly provided me with lots of comedy material.) Anna has come along with me to camps and fundraisers ever since.

Before I started attending KIDS events, I hadn't met anyone who identified as a burn survivor. Someone who has had a big impact on me is a woman named Kay Vargas. Kay has similar scars to me but is further along in life. When I met her, she struck me as being super energetic, positive, and not afraid to be in the limelight since she loves dancing so much. Kay even brought her family along to watch me perform comedy the last time I was in Sydney.

Sue and Annie

Annie and Karen

If I have to pick a favourite photo it would be this one from the finish line of the Ride4KIDS event in 2019. We cycled 550km in four days, from Byron Bay to Noosa, to raise funds, and everyone at Camp Phoenix came out to cheer us on. I'm hugging Sue Clark, who got involved through the triathlon community. I love this photo even more because in the background you'll see two of my favourite people that I've met through KIDS burns survivor Adam Boas and his wife, Jacqui Frowen.

2019 was a challenging year for me, personally. I quit my stable government job to pursue comedy, and I went through a breakup with someone who I had previously invited to do the ride with me. There were only six weeks between me getting a road bike and the event. I trained alone most days, learned how to use cleats, and had to quickly adapt to riding in a group. The photo symbolises working hard towards a goal and the immense support that the volunteers and staff at the KIDS Foundation have provided over the years.

Adam Boas once said that he wouldn't change anything, even if he had the choice to go back in time and save himself from his burns. If he hadn't gone through that, then he wouldn't have met his wife and had two beautiful kids. And how could you regret all of these wonderful things?

It's taken over a decade, but I can finally say I don't regret being burnt. I can't possibly regret all of my successes and achievements. And I certainly don't regret finding my purpose to have fun and make people feel good. I hope to bring my mum to the next Camp Phoenix so she can meet other family members who have been affected by burns and serious injuries. There's still more work to be done, especially in culturally diverse communities, to dispel the stigma and shame around burns and physical differences.

My dad passed away a few years ago, so he didn't get to see me turn things around for the better. I know he'd be proud though because, heck, I'm proud of myself. It's been eleven years since my accident, and I can confidently say I'm happier than I've ever been before scars and all.

Annie and her sister Anna (their parents wanted them to be close and that started literally by name) have become valued volunteers, taking on leadership and mentoring roles, overseeing groups of young people. Annie is an active fundraiser, donating proceeds from her gigs and of course entertaining us at camps. We have recently produced a pilot for a TV show featuring SeeMore Safety with Annie as the host and Anna is also involved. These sisters are two special people in the KIDS world.

Anna and Annie

There is something in the
human spirit that will
survive and prevail,
there is a tiny and
brilliant light burning
in the heart of man that
will not go out no matter
how dark the world becomes.

- LEO TOLSTOY

Thank you for giving me hope and my life back.

If there was ever a person to make you feel this charity was worthwhile, it would have to be this man and his beautiful, devoted wife Kendall. Kendall also holds a very special place in the KIDS Foundation family.

When Steve arrived at camp, we instantly noticed we had a challenge on our hands. He was withdrawn, showed no affection to his wife, and hardly communicated with his children. Steve was totally immersed in his suffering and self-pity. Donna Carson, as she often did, called a team meeting and set about putting plans in place to reach the real Steve. Part of the plan was to get him to go to the water hole for swimming activities that afternoon. The following morning, we saw Steve walking with his wife, holding hands. That afternoon he was playing pool with his boys, and we got to meet the most beautiful person. On the last afternoon of the camp, Steve asked to share his story with the group. Standing in front of around 120 people, I had no idea what he was about to spill out. He told us that he had planned to end his life after returning home from Camp Phoenix and this experience had changed his plans. When it was time for the last big hug, he asked what he could do to thank us. "Put in a letter what this trip has meant to you." He replied by saying, "I'm right-handed, and I have lost it, how am I supposed to do that?" "Well learn to write with your left then," I said. Sure enough, sometime later I received a handwritten letter in the mail. I shed a tear and published it in the 2004–2005 KIDS Foundation Annual Report.

Kendall and Steve

On March 10, 2005, I received a letter from Steve Harrison that read:

P.S. In the time between writing and posting this letter I was accepted back into the fitting & Machining T.A.F.E course I was doing before I burned myself

Dear Suzie & crew
I am writing this letter myself (left handed) yeah yeah I know you said I could and that is probably why I'm trying so hard.
Even you guys wouldn't believe how far I've come.
Today I finished restoring my lathe. It is now a fully functional 1.8m workshop machine that can be used for a large variety of jobs.
Not bad for a bloke with no right hand and only 20% function in his left.
Still being able to impress people is the best therapy I can imagine. Sorry, I am a born show off, I just love to see the look on peoples faces when they see what I can do.
None of this would be possible without you and the brave kids at camp Phoenix
I can rember a councilor once saying to me that coming to terms with my disabilitys would be one of the hardest things I would ever do. The kids at camp showed me that the only worthwile option was to get on with it and coming to terms was a luxury that would simply cost too much.
Disability can be a powerfull advesary but the strength in the hearts of the young who have not yet been convinced by well meaning professionals that they have a disability and the love in the hearts of people like you can be even more potent.
I belive that the success of camp Phoenix is based on treating people like people not like patients.
Well it worked for me.

I've been doing far more than I am willing to put into this letter. but as you know I joined toastmasters and I thaught you would like to hear that I am only a couple of speaches away from the level of competent Toastmaster
So let me know when I can put these new skills to use for you.

Lots of love steve Harrison.
Never lose your sense of humor.
There is no such thing as fair

My name is Steve Harrison. I am 43 years old, and I have no doubt that I would not have made it past 37 if not for the KIDS Foundation and their Burn Survivors' Network. On the 23rd of July 2002, I suffered full thickness burns to 65% of my body in a shed and house fire. I lost all the fingers on my right hand and crippled my left. The first people to be involved in saving my life were my wife Kendall and the emergency services. Next was my regional rescue helicopter, which was followed by team after team of surgeons and scores of wonderful nurses. It is not possible to easily describe what someone in my condition goes through, but a few relevant details may help.

The first things you lose apart from the obvious physical aspects are your sense of independence, dignity, hope, and a little later on, even your humanity. This occurs while you spend months laying in a bed slowly decomposing while doctors desperately try to cover the rotting parts of your body with skin grafts only to be hampered by the time it takes for the relatively healthy parts of your body to grow more skin to harvest. I looked like I had crawled out of hell and smelled like I had been dead for a week.

Every morning I had dressing changes to look forward to. These involved being taken to a room that had a bench with a drain running around it. Dressings would be removed as gently as possible, which only involved the worst agony most people ever experience and a considerable flow of bloody water in the drain around the bench. After that, it got really bad. Room temperature water slowly running over my back would be enough to make my pain medication seem like a joke. Then the coarse sponges filled with a harsh detergent called chlorhexidine were scrubbed over my newly grafted skin and my bare flesh causing a display of screaming, crying, and various guttural animal noises. I could go on, but by now you will most likely understand how easy it is to believe it is just too hard to go on living, and after fully realising your loss, that there is no point in doing so, even if you survive your current hell.

It was about this time I started receiving cards and letters from a woman named Donna Carson who had been very badly burned in an act of domestic violence. I didn't care about the cards and letters, but my wife became very interested when Donna mentioned the Burns Survivors Network and Camp Phoenix, a subsidised holiday where burns survivors and their families are able to get together and share their stories with people who understand but more importantly to share coping strategies, friendship, and support. Although by this time, I was constantly on the lookout for ways of ending my life, my wife made it abundantly clear that we were going to camp. If not for me then for the rest of the family who had been under considerable stress for the last ten months. I would have the opportunity to finish myself when we returned.

We attended camp where I refused to join in activities, avoided people as much as possible, and refused to acknowledge that any one's life could ever have hit the low that mine had regardless to what I could plainly see. Unable to avoid all activities, I found myself at a lake with the rest of the group. Children and adults were playing in the water. I noticed a small boy named Dalton sitting in his wheelchair, his burns were so severe that he could no longer use his legs, and the rest of his body had not coped much better. While I watched, he began to rock in his chair. I had no idea what he was trying to do. Then with much effort, he was able to topple his chair onto the sand then drag himself into the water and begin to play happily with the other children. It was at this point that my view on life was changed forever and I decided it wasn't over until it was over, and I still had a lot to offer.

The KIDS Foundation and Susie do nothing by halves. Within months of my visit to camp, and having learned much about my tendency to use my shed not only as a comprehensive workshop but as a sanctuary, they had arranged donations of all necessary materials for its repair. Within 18 months of my accident, I had single-handedly built a 40 m2 mezzanine floor in my shed from scrap steel, which I had to weld together. The main beam weighs 450kg, was in four pieces, spans 9 meters, and was raised 2.5m, also single-handedly. This was to prove to myself I was still capable. My shed gave me a purpose, and I was soon able to get back to creating. One of my projects was a decorative fire poker made of stainless steel, brass, and copper. I put it up for auction to raise funds for the Westpac Rescue Helicopter Service (WRHS). It raised $1350, and now framed, hanging proudly on their boardroom wall. Although I was challenged to do things differently, I still got the job done.

Since then, I have been an inspirational speaker, not only with the KIDS Foundation but for the Lions Club, local Fire Brigade, and a local school. I have also given many safety talks in industry. These talks were always performed shirtless to provide extra impact. One set of 16 presentations to the Port Waratah Coal Loader netted $52,000 per year in ongoing employee payroll deducted donations and a $100,000 yearly donation from the company itself for the WRHS. My wife and I have been charter members of the Maitland support group for the WRHS. Our group raised over $30,000 in just two years. I went on to earn a Bachelor degree in psychological science and later volunteered as a Lifeline Telephone Crisis Supporter.

In short, what the KIDS Foundation does can have huge benefits, not just for individuals and families but can reach deep into the community as well. Thank you for giving me hope and my life back.

Susie and Steve

The worst loss you've ever experienced is the greatest gift you can have.

- BYRON KATIE

Dalton

If all who have experienced Dalton's spirit do the best they can with it, then he will continue to make the world a better place.

The little boy that changed Steve's life was Dalton Moule. Dalton was a very special young person with 85% burns that overcame challenges most could not envisage. Dalton's courage, infectious smile, and "can do" attitude not only inspired many but gave others the will to live. His relentless determination brought him back to life not just once but three times. Dalton's mum Vanessa shares his story...

I had just gone to the shops, but when I arrived had forgotten my purse and had to turn around and head home to get it. I pulled up and headed into the house. Dalton jumped out and ran to his favourite play place under the house. Our house was an older Queenslander type house on stilts and had the laundry under the house. The rest of the under-house area was used for storage and had a dirt floor. Dalton had made a play area and had this weird habit of "nuding up." He didn't like wearing clothes, and the first chance he got he would take them off. It became a bit of a joke. Dalton is doing the nude thing again! So, on this particular day, he jumped out of the car, ran to his play spot, stripped off, and began playing in the dirt.

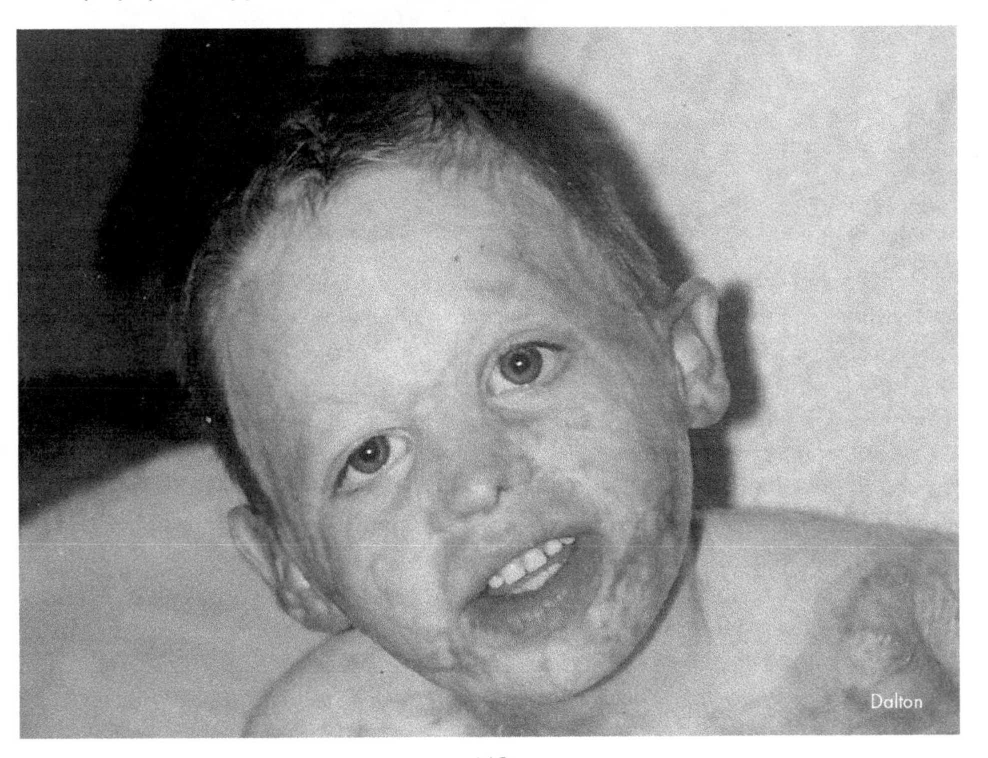

Dalton

He noticed a fuel can that had been used the day before to fill the lawn mower. Dalton picked it up and it spilt onto the ground. Close by was a gas hot water service, the fumes from the petrol ignited the pilot light, and it exploded into a ball of flames. Just as this had happened, I went down to check on Dalton and saw the flames. I ran and saw him curled up in the corner. As I picked him up, his skin peeled off, he slipped from my hands, and he dropped to the ground. The builders working next door heard all the screams and came running, called an ambulance, and kept water running over him until the ambulance arrived. Two ambulances arrived, one took Dalton to the Children's and me to the Adults as I burnt my toes and calf muscles rescuing Dalton. As soon as I could, I checked out of the Royal Brisbane and headed to the Children's to find Dalton in ICU fighting for his life. Dalton had 85% burns to his body, no other child had ever survived a burn of this degree. It would take a medical miracle for him to make it. He defied all odds and pulled through, not just once, but on three occasions. The hospital was in constant contact with an American hospital for advice. Their treatments were the most advanced, and they had more cases of survivors that had greater degree of burns than was common in Australia.

Dalton and Susie at Sea World

Dalton's burns were severe to his face, hands, arms, and legs, actually pretty much everywhere except his back. But he also lost five fingers on one hand and down to the first knuckles on the other. The treatment wasn't all that pleasant though and hard for a parent to watch, despite the fact that Dalton wasn't the sort of kid that complained. There was the physio, floating starfish, a waterbed, and a tilt table all part of Dalton's treatment. The tilt frame was used for patients to resume standing training after being confined to bed for long periods. When the blood runs into the feet, it can be very painful. The most traumatising was the frame or guard used to stretch his mouth and stop it from shrinking. Dalton just wanted to get on with whatever treatment so he could get to the games room. The funny clowns were not enough to get his attention. Actually they couldn't even get a smile out of them. He would barely be out of a full anesthetic, and he would be straight to the games room. Hospital became part of Dalton's life. He endured hundreds of operations to release tightened skin through grafts. Dalton's operations continued right up until the weekend of our camping trip. We often went on camping trips taking either quad bikes or fishing gear. The boy's hobbies included the Xbox, fishing, and motocross. My dad owned the Black Duck Valley Motocross Park, and it was part of the boy's life. Dalton had his own quadbike and rode it with no fear.

On this occasion, we had just picked Dalton up from hospital. He had had skin grafts to his under arm, and his arm was in a splint in a right angle from his shoulder out. Dalton was keen to get home and take part in a camping trip we were looking forward to. The cars were packed, and we headed off on our fishing trip. We had a fabulous weekend fishing and spending time with the boys. Dalton's highlight was catching some sort of shark/ray.

The last photo ever taken of Dalton

On the way home, I travelled in my car with Dalton and our other son Declan. Scott (the boy's father) was travelling in the four-wheel drive behind with the camping and fishing gear. On this particular day, we travelled across a causeway, as we do regularly, but on this occasion, we were hit unexpectedly by a surge of water from a heavy downpour upstream carrying our car into the river. Scott travelling in the car behind us followed our car along the bank to where it became wedged against a tree. Scott jumped out and grabbed Declan and took him to safety and came back for Dalton. I quickly removed Dalton's splint to get him out of the car, but as I did, another surge of water came toward us, picked us up, and took us further downstream. We grabbed a tree and held on until Scott got back to us, but as he did, I turned around to find Dalton was no longer hanging onto that tree. He was not in sight. Later his body was found downstream. Dalton had drowned.

It is tragic enough to have your child fall from your arms once, but a second time is unimaginable. On February 6, 2010, Dalton sadly lost his life in a tragic accident in Gatton, near Toowoomba. Dalton's funeral was a very sad occasion but special celebration of his life. I can remember talking to his burn surgeon at his funeral, who literally had run from surgery to ensure he didn't miss the service. By this I mean he pulled back his suit jacket to reveal his white shirt splattered in blood. Steve Harrison, who accounts Dalton as a reason of saving his life, sent me a letter to express his sadness.

This letter was read at Dalton's funeral. February 10, 2010.

I have been saddened by the recent news of Dalton's accident. I know you are attending Dalton's funeral, and I would be grateful if you would pass on my thoughts to his family.

I never knew Dalton well. In fact, I probably only tried to talk to him five or six times. Sometimes he smiled and spoke, sometimes he shied away. After all, who was this bloke who came at him with such words as "proud" and "inspirational"? He didn't know much about these things; he was just Dalton. But we all know he was much more than that.

He was a spirit, brighter and stronger than most, after all, you don't go through what Dalton went through without having something amazing inside. I suppose I can only speak of the side of Dalton I saw from the sidelines.

The first time I saw Dalton was a little over twelve months after a serious burns accident of my own. I was still a mass of painful, still healing wounds with many months of excruciating surgeries ahead of me. I had already given up. I believed my fate was worse than anything anyone else had ever had to endure. I was only at Camp Phoenix under sufferance. I believed life was no longer worth living, and this was leading me to an inevitable and irreversible decision.

I saw many people at Camp Phoenix who had been burned to varying degrees. Only a few approached the level of injury I had suffered and even fewer looked like they could have had worse. Dalton was one of these people. Though I saw these people getting on with their lives and catching up with friends they only saw at camp, this did not affect the decision I had made.

I even recall watching Dalton who was confined to his chair with his friends running around him still being able to laugh and play. I sat and watched this for a few minutes thinking sad thoughts on Dalton's behalf, but even after I hobbled away consumed in my own cloud of misery and defeat, Dalton played on.

I managed to avoid most people and activities, but eventually found myself on the bank of a lake where adults sat and watched children splashing, squealing, playing, and generally having a great time. I noticed Dalton sitting in his chair on the bank, legs wrapped in plastic, watching his friends having a great time. I began having sad thoughts on Dalton's behalf, this time thinking of all the things he would never do again.

While I was burying myself in this dark cloud, Dalton begun to rock his chair from side to side. I worried he would fall out, but I was in no condition to do anything about it. Then finally and with a thud, he and his chair went sideways onto the sand, and then slowly he dragged himself down the bank and into the water where he began playing with his friends. His friends didn't think this was unusual, after all, it was just Dalton.

My life was changed. I believe at that moment I was given a great gift. It was a tiny piece of Dalton's spirit. It was not something Dalton would miss nor would he ever know he had given it to me. After all, it was something that radiated from him constantly.

Over the years, I made many friends at Camp Phoenix and noted that particularly those who would have needed it most had the same gift, and that often made me wonder. We all knew and admired that little boy, he was infectious.

I have a feeling that there are a great many people affected by Dalton's spirit, and the world could only be a better place for him having been visited by it. I myself have tried to do good things since I was given my second chance, helping others when I can. I have also been called inspirational and have been told that people view their lives differently after meeting me.

That was not me before my accident, that was not me before meeting Dalton. I am sure that the small part of Dalton I carry with me helps me be a better person and that he has affected many other people in the same way. Last year, I gave nearly forty safety talks to well over a thousand people. I included the story of what Dalton had done for me in every talk and was told by many people that they had found it inspirational. I am sure those who were closest to Dalton will miss him greatly, but as a person who has been close enough to death to see it's brilliance and feel it's calming and tranquil embrace only to be torn back into this cruel world we find ourselves in, I say do not mourn him.

I am not a religious man, but I believe Dalton is currently resting in a far better place. I also believe a soul such as Dalton's once rested will not stay away for long as the world needs such spirits if it is to heal. If all who have experienced Dalton's spirit do the best they can with it, then he will continue to make the world a better place, and I cannot think of a better way to honour his memory.

Best wishes, Steve Harrison

Whenever you find yourself
doubting how far you can go,
just remember how far you have come.
Remember everything you have faced,
all the battles you have won,
and all the fears you have overcome.

- N.R. WALKER

CHAPTER FIVE

Strength

In families not so well-designed to perform in the best interests of children, it is remarkable how the children can find inner strength to submerge into survival mode. Sadly, abuse and family dysfunction is relatively common when it comes to the lives of many that come into the KIDS Foundation family. Long-term effects can have a great and lasting influence on their emotional state and how they relate to others.

On the morning of the last day of the camp that changed Steve's life, I decided to go for an early morning walk. It had been a pretty emotional camp, and I needed some "me" time. I hadn't gone too far along the beach when I heard a voice say, "Is it okay if I come for a walk with you?" "Of course," I said. This was a young girl we will call Kari for the purpose of this story. I had spent most of my time with the younger children at this camp and hadn't had a chance to get to know her. "Please, come and join me, Kari. I see you are here on your own. That is a brave thing for a 15-year-old girl to do," I said. "Yes, my good mum would have been proud of me," she said. Now, this was an interesting response, I thought. "Your good Mum," I repeated it. "Yes," she said, and then went on to tell me her story.

I learned that when
life pulls you under,
you can kick
against the bottom,
break the surface
and breathe again.

- SHERYL SANDBERG

Kari

If I had some understanding of how fast, fierce, and ferocious fuel could ignite, I would not have hung around to ask Mum what she was doing.

At the age of 10, my parents separated, so I went to live with my mum who suffered with very severe mental health issues. This illness was greatly affecting her will to be a parent and leaving her with the impossible task of looking after her own wellbeing, let alone a child. She had so many personalities as well. I thought I could tell when she was having a bad day, but on this occasion, it took me by surprise.

We sat down on the couch and watched the movie Titanic together. In conversation, I told her that when we were in our German class that day, we saw a fire through the window of our portable classroom. I remember it being a very hot sunny day, and the guy across the road went to start his lawn mower, which caught on fire. It then spread and set the grass and fence on his property alight. I had no idea that it was to lead to something that was going to occur that evening and that was going to change my life forever. When Titanic finished, I went off to my room. I didn't think anything was out of the ordinary. It was some time before I fell asleep. Then I woke up to a loud crashing and banging noise. I got up and found Mum had thrown furniture into the hallway and was pouring petrol over it. She then picked up the phone and called my father. When my father answered the phone, she shouted something at him. He knew my mother was in one of her moods that night and feared the worst for me. He told me later that that night he heard the emergency chopper fly over the house, not knowing it was actually me being flown to the hospital.

After she hung up the phone call, I asked her what she was doing. She then got the can of petrol and splashed more petrol towards me. I was in a confined space at the entrance near the front door. The petrol, the whole 10 litres of it, landed close by onto the floor just inside the doorway. This is a horrific experience I want to share, forever buried at the back of my mind. I had no idea of how dangerous petrol can be. What happened to me next, happened in about three to five seconds. It was unbelievabley quick. My mother had lit a match, it sparked, and without it even touching the floor, the vapour of the petrol ignited the whole room instantly. An orange flash ripped around us as quickly as you turn on the switch of a light. The whole confined space lit up, and the noise that followed was deafening. Then there was an explosion. You could hear air burning extremely fast, it was traumatising.

It is hard to explain and for someone to imagine, as not that many people have experienced such a traumatic experience, except some of the kids I have met through the KIDS Foundation. But one thing is for sure, if I had some understanding of how fast, fierce, and ferocious fuel could ignite, I would not have hung around to ask Mum what she was doing. I would have exited the house immediately before my mum was able to strike a match. Now that the match was lit, all I could do was get out of the house. It took me just a few seconds to get to the door, open the first door, and open the security door. Luck was with me that evening because the door was not locked with the key; it saved my life. Had the security door not been open, I definitely would not have survived. It was as simple as that. I flung it open and jumped out and rolled down the driveway. I did what I was taught in school back then, and that was to stop, drop, and roll. However, I made the mistake of not to keep rolling on the flames burning on my back.

My pants were completely burnt away, my legs were charcoal, barbecue black, and my toes curled upwards and pointed towards the ceiling (similar to when you cook raw prawns and the muscle curls with the heat), and my face was burnt. I tried to put water on my legs and wash it off with the tap water out the front while awaiting the ambulance. To my dismay, the black did not wash off. I was in utter shock. The only parts of my body that were not burnt were my upper thighs, stomach, and back. Miraculously, my face and neck were burnt but had first degree burns and made a full recovery. Everything exposed was burnt. My hands had sort of melted, and the hand that opened the door left an imprint on it. I looked down and panicked. When I was outside lying at the bottom of the driveway, I was sure I was going to die that night. I thought maybe there was a tiny bit of hope of survival if I made it to hospital in time.

Because of my age and the extent of the damage caused by the burns, I was taken by ambulance to the nearest regional town with a hospital and flown from there to the Royal Children's Hospital in Melbourne (RCH). I remember in the helicopter being given high doses of morphine and ice to suck on. The trip took around 45 minutes to reach the RCH. The helicopter I was transported in was an emergency chopper with a lot of medical equipment. After arriving at the hospital, I can't remember much as I was put into an induced coma and spent some time in intensive care. Then I was moved to a ward where I spent a good three months.

Another three months of out-patient treatment followed before I made a full recovery, well to the best of my body's capability considering the burns were so severe. My recovery was all about operations, very high pain killers, a whole team of professional nurses and doctors, specialists, and cleaning staff, and the most expensive blow-up bed at the hospital. The trainee nurses didn't come to visit me, but they would come past my room to observe the bed I was on or the bath used to wash my burns. The bath was used for me and others with burns to remove the dead skin. Everything was painful, the baths, the dressings, physio, and the compression body suits, which were awful and made me feel really hot during summer.

Despite the painful times, I did have a few special moments during my time in the RCH. It was not the clowns in the Starlight centre or that macadamia hand puppet show that aired to entertain the kids. It was a special person who bought me the biggest bunch of flowers I have ever seen. One of the welfare nurses explained to me I was going to have a special visitor. She mentioned her name, but I had never heard the name before she visited me in the children's hospital that day. This special person was none other than Kaz Cooke. I had no idea how famous she was until my dad and others talked about her coming to visit and then sometime later when I came across her books.

When you don't have a mum around, sometimes asking a complete stranger about these topics can be awkward, so to be able to have someone through easy-to-read books tell you the gooey stuff is fantastic. I hope Kaz gets to read this book so I can say a big thank you to her. Her kindness was something I will never forget. I remember at the time thinking how much my room filled with these beautiful flowers reminded me of my childhood. I used to watch romper room as a kid and loved the bee and the noise it made. Someone had given me a bee toy, and I used to carry it with me everywhere. It has been a long time, so I am unsure whether she will remember me or not. I definitely remember her though.

The incident happened in the same year, but a month or so before the 9/11 terrorist attacks in 2001. It was after my first operation I looked up at the tiny TV in the top corner of my room and saw flashing news of planes flying into the twin tower buildings in America. I thought, "What is happening?" "Why is it flashing over the news every two minutes?" My dad came in and said to me, "At least you are lucky you are alive. You would not believe what is happening in the world right now. People are jumping out of high-rise story buildings." I then worked it out, that what I was seeing repeatedly on TV was a terrorist attack in America. Fire had ripped through some of the buildings, and many people died and many others had been left with severe burns. I thought to myself, "I am lucky to be alive, and I would not have had any knowledge about it and everything else going on in the world, had I not survived that day." Strangely, I thought of things like this, how fortunate I was.

One day, the welfare nurse came into my room and mentioned about the KIDS Foundation's camps and how they would be good for me. That is how I met Susie. One morning I saw her walking along the beach at a camp on Moreton Island, and I asked her if I could walk with her. She thought I was brave to go to the camp on my own. She asked how I was coping. The rest is history.

I have been part of the Burn Survivors' Network run by the KIDS Foundation for quite some time now. I have met so many different burn survivors, some with petrol burns, chemical burns, with severe burns from hot baths, people spilling hot liquids on themselves accidently, people who have been burnt in bush fires, people who have had petrol thrown on them by a jealous lover, people burnt in car accidents who lost their entire family (them being the only lone survivor), from playing with matches, and from abuse and burn survivors that received their injuries from a parent, like I did. Their individual stories are different from mine, but we have all had traumatic experiences related to fire or abuse.

One Christmas holidays, Susie invited me to join her family on their holiday at the Murray River. I remember Susie's husband Brett because he was an incredible driver. He drove us to the camp site on dirt tracks. He definitely had done plenty of four-wheel driving before, very experienced. Susie reassured us her husband would get us there safe and sound, and get us there he did. We went through a section that was quite boggy on the river's edge. I was sure we were going to get stuck and all have to get out of the vehicle and push. But he moved the car back and forward and got it out. It was a real four-wheel drive experience, absolutely amazing. She married an utter champion. Susie and Brett and their kids are top athletes and had generously organised a bike for me through Giant so I could join them on their rides. Every morning we would get up and ride sometimes for hours. I got to spend lots of time with Susie and chat to her about things that helped me decide on choices for my future. One of them was to get fit and take an interest in my health, which I continue to do today.

Some years later, still interested in sports, I enrolled in a Sports and Recreation Diploma, a three-year TAFE course. I graduated in 2009 and then went on to do an advanced course to gain an Athletes Support Diploma in 2010. The sporting industry job opportunities didn't provide a steady income for me, so I settled for a job in a warehouse working for an organisation providing services for the Government.

One time at a Ballarat kids only camp, we were visited by one of the Australian road cyclist teams, Drapac. They were racing that weekend in Ballarat, and we got to watch them. The event had a community ride I was keen to do it, mind you I hardly knew how to ride a bike at this stage. It was before I was exposed to the O'Neill family rides. I was full of adventure and wanted to explore and see Ballarat where my idol (Susie) works. Susie found me a bike and an outfit, and I headed off. Boy was the ride tough. I found it harder than it seemed, looking at it on paper. As I reached the top of the hill, the sun was blaring in my eyes. I now understood why Susie wore those ridiculous looking sunglasses she wore on the bike. The bike riding experience was really enjoyable, but the uphill bits were slow. I left going fast for the professionals as they sped past. I didn't know anything about gears until that day. The bike stayed in the big gear the whole time because I didn't know how to change it. No wonder I was falling behind up the hills. I finished, but not as I would have liked, especially the fact that I rode a sluggish mountain bike in a big gear the whole way. It was still an experience I will never forget. I never will forget the kids encouraging words and cheering for me at the finish line.

"Thanks guys! You are the legends," I called. That was a special day for me; I felt so included and supported by a group of special friends. I felt I had secured a place within this group—I was part of the KIDS family.

All I can say is without the blame of any individuals, much more could have been done even to prevent what happened to me on that particular day. I felt I had been let down by professional authorities who were aware of my mother's condition. One night, I was on my own because they took my mum to the hospital. I was left alone for the whole night, too young to be on my own. In the morning, I got a phone call from my mum, who was still in the hospital, to say I was to look after myself, to go to school on my own, cook for myself, and manage as best I could. I was so scared going to sleep on my own in a lonely cold house. But sometimes I had to hide. I had little choice but to stay away when mum was bad and unbearable. I was so scared to come home. I didn't want anyone to know. I would run away and beg a friend whom I knew from school whose mum also with a mental illness, if I could stay the night at her house. Sometimes I would get teased by other kids at school about my hygiene. But I couldn't go home to get clean, have a shower, wash my clothes, or get food. I didn't want to be taken away or go to a foster home or to someone I didn't know to take proper care of me.

Kari was one of the many young people that really made my heart ache. For a 15-year-old girl to lose her mum at a time when there are lots of womanhood questions to be answered is a really tough time. She needed someone in her life she could trust that would help her ease the transition into adulthood. Kari was maturing into a young woman with very little female support around her. I couldn't have been more eager to do something to prevent the overwhelming circumstances of growing up and simply make Kari's life better.

Back to the walk along the beach ... Kari said, "It is not the burns that is troubling me - I have lost the good mum I knew, I have moved in with my dad I hardly know, I have a new councillor, I'm at a new school, and how am I meant to make friends when I look like this?" She then showed me her scarred legs. "My whole world has been turned upside down." We walked and talked some more about her hobbies and things she liked doing. I learned about her love for badminton and other sporting talents. I asked if she had ever been hurt by her mum in the past. Kari explained that on one occasion her mum lost control and slid the table towards her head as she was crouching in the corner on the floor cowering from her mother's outburst of rage. The next day she went to school and the school nurse sent her via ambulance to the local hospital to get it checked. She was then taken away from her mum and went to live with her grandparents for a short time because her dad was working. She reminded me she had been pretty good at gauging when her bad mum personalities were about to appear. I was also curious to know what support she had been given from authorities and her school.

The KIDS Foundation had become a regular beneficiary and preferred charity partner of many triathlons and cycling events. On one particular occasion, we combined a KIDS only camp with a cycling event that had come to Ballarat. The Drapac Porsche Cycling Team was one of the KIDS Foundation's passionate donors and arranged for the children to take joy rides over the weekend in their Porsche showcase cars. The cyclists came to the camp to meet the children and shared some cycling tips. Kari was so inspired she asked if she could take part in the community ride the next day. We found a mountain bike for her to ride, Drapac organised a cycling kit, and she headed off on a 20km ride not having had any training or real preparation.

I was unaware she had never been on a bike with gears. After quite a few of the 20km riders had returned and others were flooding through, I became a bit worried, because I knew how strong she was. Kari had displayed quite good sporting abilities during camp activities, and we expected she would have returned by now. Then we saw her coming toward the finish line with the greatest smile. The children were flying flags, waving pompoms, and cheering her on. I noticed she had the chain on a big gear. She told us she didn't know how to change gears so she just kept riding! That pretty much sums up Kari and her determination and strength to keep going.

The following Christmas, I invited Kari on our family holiday on the Murray River. Our holidays always included quite a bit of riding because we were always training for an up-and-coming triathlon or Ironman event. So, the road bikes are an essential packing item. Kari took her mountain bike as well. She had developed a love for cycling and was quite a strong rider. Giant had generously organised a bike for her. Each morning we would get up at around 5 a.m. and usually head out in the dark on the road before the traffic started to build. She would be right there beside us; she wasn't missing out on any opportunity to ride and on occasions kept up with the road bikes.

One afternoon, we were chatting about Donna's book, which Kari had found inspirational and reassuring, considering she had experienced some of the trauma. She shared with me the fact that she was not supposed to have contact with her mum, however, her mum had sent her a Christmas present. Kari pulled out a box. In the box was a card, a lovely letter, a small gift, and a tape. I got out the tape recorder, which was the recording and playing device in those days, put the tape in, and pressed play. It was a recording her mum had made to send her a special message. I wasn't ready for what was to come next. The voice completely changed from the "good Mum" to the "bad Mum" Kari had described in the past. That chilling voice still haunts me to this day.

Children deserve nurturing families and environments in which their physical, emotional, educational, and social needs are met. It is remarkable how some children deal with such trauma, especially when they don't have a secure family support network around them. Kari comes to a camp when she can, or I give her a call to see how she is going. We text often and I constantly think about Kari, her strength, courage, and how the simple things in life mean the world to her.

KIDS

It took me a long
time not to judge
myself through
someone else's eyes.

- SALLY FIELD

To survive abuse, a lightning strike, and then to be rescued from a burning house, as they say, Sally's time was not up.

Sally is a strong female role model who inspires others, like Kari. She gives those who are often overlooked a voice. Sally has had her fair share of trauma and uses the KIDS platform to help others gain the courage they need to face their new world and the strength to get there.

I grew up with two older sisters, my mother, and, well let's call him "the sperm donor." I can't bring myself to find a term to describe this person. It's painful for me to think about it. Let's say my childhood was not a pleasant one. I was unable to learn at school because I was distracted by what was happening at home. One time I was injured at school and was taken to hospital. I tried to make out that I was worse than I really was so I could stay in hospital and not have to go home. I remember running away once to my friend's house down the road. She hid me in her shed for days and bought me leftover food until her mother realised where the roast spuds had gone, and I had to return home.

My sister and I were often bullied by the seven Davies boys down the road. On one occasion, my eldest sister had her head smashed into the train window by the boys because our father's drunken behaviour had kept them up all night. The low self-esteem that develops from a dysfunctional upbringing can be irreversible. It was my utmost ambition to give my children a happy childhood, where they know they are loved and valued. I went through my childhood always feeling like I never belonged. Horrible memories often come flooding back, like the time we were living at Nanny's when "the sperm donor" broke into the house with a gun and pointed it at us. The terror in my eyes as I looked down the barrel of the gun, my mum says, made him stop. I loved my nan; she made me feel special. We would often stay there when mum left him on and off. Sometimes we would hide in the shed, and when he found us, he would march us back into the house single file, like we were in the army.

At the age of sixteen, I got my first job working at Kmart and then in a supermarket. One day, I went to collect the trolleys outside the supermarket. At the time, there was a storm brewing. All of a sudden, my left hand was thrown off the handle of the trolley, the right stuck to it, and a big bang went through my head. I was taken to get checked out, and tests revealed I had been struck by lightning. This incident has led me to experience epileptic fits at times throughout my life. I suffered three fits in the first year of being diagnosed. Then they became more frequent.

One day I was invited to attend Moomba with a work friend, her brother, and their neighbour. The moment I met their neighbour Mark we were hooked. We really loved each other, so much. I married Mark some years later, and we had two beautiful children, James and Brittney. Our marriage didn't last, but we have remained best mates. I blame myself for our marriage break-up; there was too much childhood baggage that got in the way. Mark was a beautiful husband and the most kind-hearted and understanding man I had ever met. I can't tell you how many times the kids called their dad to come home because of my seizures. He had very understanding bosses. As James and Brittney grew older, they became wonderful carers after watching their father take good care of me. They are great mates to this day, and I couldn't be prouder of them.

I was beginning to fall apart when I left Mark. And then things got worse, to a point I had a nervous breakdown. After leaving Mark, I rented a house in Mill Park. It wasn't great, but we made it into a home. It had a few issues, one being a faulty gas heater that I spoke to the agents about on several occasions. It hadn't been fixed when on the May 24, 2003, the heater exploded, and the house caught on fire. A group of young boys were walking by the house and raised the alarm. The fire brigade arrived in minutes, and I was rescued. I was found unconscious lying on the bed in a smoke-filled room. I was rushed to the Alfred Hospital. On arrival, all my long blonde hair was shaved off, and I was put in a medically induced coma. There I stayed for seven months, most of that was in ICU. I had to learn to walk, eat, and talk again even with a tracheotomic tube in my throat.

It has been 18 years since I was trapped in my burning home. In the first four months of hospitalisation, I died five times. I received 35% burns to my body and lung damage, and I lost five fingers, my gall bladder, and a section of my bowel as a result of one of the many infections. The experience has also left me with Post Traumatic Stress Disorder (PTSD) and clinical depression.

A number of years ago, I had the absolute pleasure of meeting the fireman that saved my life. There were quite a few tears that day on both sides. As I began the recovery journey, I needed to know there was hope. I didn't want pity or people feeling sorry for me, I needed to feel like I was living, not just existing. The beautiful nurse that was looking after me told be about the Burn Survivors' Network run by the KIDS Foundation. This program was for families, and therefore adults were welcome as well.

Zoi, Sally, Bev and Eliza

When I returned home, I jumped on the internet and checked it out. I liked what I saw. There was a camp coming up, so I booked in. My family were quite nervous about me reacting so quickly and thought it was too much of a rushed decision. It turned out to be the best rushed decision I have ever made. What I took away from my first camp gave me strength, hope, and confidence to move forward. The KIDS Foundation helped me to find my soul again and give me purpose. There I met Susie O'Neill, and we have since become good friends. I have now been with this wonderful charity for over 14 years. I have got to know all the kids, their families, and other adult survivors. I have become a mentor for some of the young girls at camp and attended many KIDS functions and fundraisers where I help out selling raffle tickets and doing whatever I can to give back.

Camp TANGO Hamilton Island

Since finding the KIDS Foundation, I have taken on many things that I otherwise would not have done. I have learned that there is always someone worse off. I remember a girl in rehab who only ever had one visitor, her brother. She wore hospital clothes because she had none of her own. I gave her a pair of my pants and a pink top. She was overwhelmed, and her eyes lit up with joy. She looked so pretty in her new outfit. My family were a little taken back when they saw her wearing my clothes, especially considering I had lost everything in the fire and the only things I had to my name were a few clothes my family bought me, and here I was giving it away.

Sally at Camp TANGO Hamilton Island

That was Sally, one of the kindest and most treasured ladies that have come into the Foundation. She is funny, has great people skills, and is very good at crafts despite only having five fingers. Sally has volunteered and mentored young survivors at many camps. On one flight to a camp that was sponsored by Hamilton Island Resort, Sal began chatting to a lady beside her on the plane who was quite curious about our group. It turned out she ran the water sports on the island and invited us to come down and experience the fun water activities, free of charge. There was no way we could have otherwise afforded to participate. The children had the best day, and that was where Matt Thiele tackled his fear of water and took a ride on the biscuit. Sally has given me the most meaningful little gifts and messages that remain etched in my mind and that are gathered in my special memory box. What Sal has been through is more than most can imagine. Her resilience and strength to overcome the challenges life has thrown her is admirable to say the least. Other survivors have such an insightful impact on the recovery of others. Sally shares this poem written for her by a fellow burn survivor.

Stand Up and Be Proud

There is nothing wrong with who you are or what you do.
Don't let others become the judge of you.

Let them understand that we are all unique.
If they stop and stare, then let them peek.

If anything, curiosity is the reason why
they find it hard to just walk by.
Don't let us judge them; it's not their sin because
they may only know of smooth skin.

Their imagination must run wild.
The thought of our life exiled.

But we need to teach them our story is so brave.
How our life is just as precious to save.

If we let them know we did no wrong.
Show them that we were still strong.

They will stand beside us with hearts of gold.
Remembering the courage that they were told.

Don't let us shy from who we are.
Don't starve the world from one less star.

Cause we are special no matter what was done.
Stand up and be proud of who you have become.

By Kelly McMillan

The bond that binds
us is beyond choice.
We are brothers.
We are brothers in
what we share.

-URSULA K. LE GUIN

The day their mum's trust was shattered

We had heard of this horrific story on the news where two children were burnt in a car fire, set alight by their father. It is incomprehensible how a parent could inflict pain on their own child and the cruelty of the injuries we see of children who survive.

This is a story that no one wants to read or hear about. More than a tragic story though, it is a story about young brothers who have a much-loved, wonderful mum, each other, their loyal friends, extended family, and a supportive school. They have inner strength that demonstrates their resilience and positive attitude to life.

The boys were flown to the Royal Children's Hospital in Melbourne (RCH) in critical condition. Eight-year old Fletcher suffered burns to 23% of his body; five-year old Spencer had burns to 37% of his body, including full thickness burns to his shoulders and neck. Their mum tells how she always considered herself a positive, happy person, but one day she realised she was not as happy as she could be...

Spencer and Fletcher

On December 3, 2012, I left my marriage of nearly 13 years. Unfortunately, I was unable to take my children, Fletcher (then aged 8) and Spencer (then aged 5), with me. I trusted my now ex-husband to care for them until I had somewhere to live and we could arrange shared care. Sadly, I learned I should never have trusted him.

On the evening of December 5, 2012, my ex picked Fletcher and Spencer up from after school care and day-care and took them home. He told the boys to stay in the car and gave them their favourite teddy bears and a bag of lollies. They had so much trust in their father, they did as he asked them. Meanwhile, he loaded three gas bottles into the car boot and turned them on. He then got back in the car, shut the door, and proceeded to light up a cigarette. I believe the results of the open flame and the gas leaking into the car were almost immediate, and the car caught on fire. While all this was happening, I was at a friend's house, waiting to go and collect my boys to have them for the weekend. Instead, I had a phone call from a police officer to say my children had been involved in a fire. I immediately knew this wasn't an accident. My ex-husband had done this out of spite! I couldn't believe that a father could do this to his own children. He is supposed to love them unconditionally.

The next few months were a blur. We spent five and a half months in hospitals. Fletcher and Spencer had many surgeries, skin grafts, tracheotomies, dressing changes, etc. Both boys had to learn to talk, stand, walk, and even eat again. I was determined we would get through this. It's just a twist in the path of life. We were eventually discharged from hospital and could go home and back to a somewhat normal life. We developed a new normal of doctors and specialist appointments and settled into our life.

My ex-husband was charged with two accounts of attempted murder and found guilty. He was sentenced to 20 years prison with a non-parole period of 15 years. He appealed the head sentence, which was denied, however he did have the non-parole period reduced to 12 years.

As time went on, my children were happy, and I was generally happy, but when the boys went to bed of a night, I missed the company of another adult. I turned to the internet and a dating app and chatted to a few different men, but none of them seemed quite right, and I would soon fob them off or they would soon learn I was the mother of the little boys that got burnt. Eventually, there was just one man left. His name was Christian. We would speak for hours on the telephone and send each other messages. We decided to meet, and eventually he met my boys also. There was an immediate connection between Christian and Spencer. Fletcher took a bit longer to come around to this man being in our lives.

We attended our first KIDS Foundation camp in August 2013, and it was there that I opened up and spoke about what happened for the very first time. We felt at home with these amazing group of survivors and KIDS Foundation staff and volunteers. The Foundation is our second family and has helped my sons gain confidence.

Spencer and Fletcher

Christian and I married in 2016, and we continue to attend the camps, which we all enjoy. I remember early on when the boys were still in hospital, Fletcher turned to me and said, "Why did Dad do this to us?" It took my breath away at first, but I stopped and thought and then said to Fletcher, "Sometimes when we are angry, we say and do things we don't always mean." Fletcher contemplated this and then said, "Dad made a bad choice, didn't he?" I didn't need to answer him, Fletcher already knew the answer. We all make choices in life, and I made the choice to find happiness. Regardless of what has happened, I have found my happiness in my children, my husband Christian, and my extended family. That's my choice.

When Fletcher and Spencer's father was arrested, would you believe, he pleaded not guilty. The sentencing judge found their father had decided to kill his sons to spite his wife, who had recently left him. He was sentenced to 20 years in prison, with a non-parole period of 15 years. To make matters worse, he appealed the sentences, arguing both periods were excessive and disproportionate to his offending. The Crown prosecutor argued the sentence was justified because the crime was premeditated to cause death to two young children and to take revenge on someone else. He said he was not remorseful, and the sentence was not excessive. However, Tasmania's

Criminal Court of Appeal was divided on whether to allow the appeal, with two justices in favour of cutting the non-parole period to 12 years, believing it was unlikely he would reoffend given the crime was related to family circumstances. He will be out in the year 2024.

Camp Phoenix

I can remember the day we gained Alison's trust to care for her boys' needs emotionally as well as physically, applying dressings, pressure garments, and a neck brace. It was at a Camp TANGO, which is normally just for children and young people, however we often allow a parent or support person to attend until the children's confidence has increased and we have earned their trust. We were at a holiday park on the Victorian coastline when Alison came up and asked how we would feel if she left the boys with us. Christian was attending a conference in Melbourne, and she hadn't had time to herself for quite some time, always putting the boys needs first. Her parents, the boy's grandparents, were amazing support for Alison, but the treatment the boys were undergoing was painful and taking a toll on her.

It is traumatic for a parent to have to constantly inflict that level of pain and discomfort on their own child, although knowing it is for the best if they are to have a better quality of life. Of course, we encouraged Alison to go and were honoured that she had bestowed her trust in us. I think that weekend was a real turning point for the boys. They engaged fully with the group and connected with their "buddies." This is the first time the boys had been buddied up with male mentors, and that in itself was a big deal. The last time Alison had left the boys with a male figure was the time their lives were changed forever. This was a man that was thought of as a loving father. Their mum tells how the boys "worshipped the ground their father walked on. They often told their dad that they loved him, and he would reciprocate, saying he loved them too."

Last year, Fletcher and Spencer were visited by Governor-General David Hurley and presented with medallions he gives out at his discretion to celebrate individuals.

Camp Phoenix RACV Noosa

Despite their injuries and challenges, they are getting on with life and overcoming what they experienced in 2012 at the hands of their father. The boys are dedicated Sydney Swans fans. KIDS have been able to arrange special meet and greet opportunities with the players, and they have often been invited into the clubrooms. Alison couldn't be prouder of them and how they are handling life. "They are giving life a real hard go. I've told them not to expect anything from anyone, and if you want something, you've got to go and get it yourselves." Her two sons have grown into beautiful, likeable, caring and funny young men. Spencer has a cheeky sense of humour. He tells us he wants to be a professional "doughnut tester" later in life. It is part of a survivor's life, especially with facial burns, to deal with the staring, and some will just ask what happened. A young person recently asked Spencer, "What happened to you?" He replied, "I went half way to hell."

Alison, Christian, Spencer and Fletcher at Camp Phoenix

Sadly, at any one time about one third of the children we support have been injured by a parent or through an act of abuse or crime, often under the most horrific circumstances involving burns from either fire or boiling water.

One moment can
change a day,
one day can change a life,
and one life can
change the world.

- BUDDHA

The unimaginable happened, again.

You are sure to remember the story of the out-of-control car that sped through a day-care centre changing the lives of two families forever. On December 15, 2003, Sophie Delezio and Molly Wood were badly injured when a car crashed through a child-care centre window in Sydney. The girls, two years of age at the time, were trapped under the car, which caught on fire. Sophie suffered burns to 85% of her body and lost fingers on one hand, both feet, and her right ear. If one traumatic accident wasn't enough for a little body to deal with, then the unimaginable happened again. Two and a half years later, on May 5, 2006, Sophie was once again badly injured in a road accident. Sophie was being pushed across a crossing by her nanny in a wheelchair when she was hit by a car and thrown into the air. Her injuries were horrific, fractured ribs, a tear to her left lung, numerous broken bones, and bruises, as well as suffering a heart attack.

Following Sophie's first incident, her parents founded the Day of Difference Foundation, a charity dedicated to raising funds for research into paediatric burns. That is how we got to meet Kel. The Delezios attended a Camp Phoenix the KIDS Foundation had organised just outside Sydney. It is very rewarding when charities that share core values and purpose can collaborate to further a cause.

Sarah, Susie, Sophie and Teneille

*Things work out best
for those who make
the best of how
things work out.*

- JOHN WOODEN

Living as a burn survivor hasn't been easy...

At the same camp, the Delezios sponsored Kel's family to come along. Kel is a remarkable young man that has a love of sports and high ambitions, he tells his story:

When I was 12 months old, my birth mum held me in a bath of boiling water. Once she realised how badly she had hurt me, she called an ambulance. The ambulance rushed me to Griffith Hospital (out in the country). My injuries were far too severe for a small hospital, so I was air lifted from Griffith to Westmead Hospital. I was told I died a few times on my way to Westmead, in the fixed wing aircraft, and was bought back to life. Once I arrived at the hospital and my injuries were assessed, I needed some of my toes and fingers amputated, as they were so severely burnt. To this day, I've had 100+ operations from skin grafts to skin releases. When I was released from hospital, I went to live with my new family. I was fostered out after the incident to a family who later adopted me. They have been a tremendous support and have got me through many challenges throughout my life.

Living as a burn survivor hasn't been easy. There's been bullying, judgement, and the stares just to name a few. The thing that makes me annoyed most is when people just see me as a burn victim. I don't want them to feel bad for me. I am on this earth for a reason and live my life to the fullest. Without sounding corny or cliché, without sustaining these injuries, I wouldn't have been able to be a mentor and been able to find the KIDS Foundation. The Foundation to me is more of a family then a foundation. We all know what the other members have been through and are one strong united family.

In 2011, I was lucky enough to be given access to an AFL corporate box at the SCG with the Delezio family. That's where I had the pleasure of meeting Luke Power. It was a few weeks after he "retired" from the Brisbane Lions, and there were rumours about him joining the newest AFL team, which was based in Blacktown close to where I was living. I struck up a conversation with Luke and discussed how I knew the Delezio family and then just let him enjoy the footy game. A few weeks later, Luke was announced as an inaugural member of the GWS Giants AFL team. I then started supporting my "local" team and attended their first ever fan day out at Rouse Hill where I went up to Luke and reintroduced myself. There was absolutely no need to as he said, "G'day Kel, good to see you again." We spent about 20 minutes chatting all while he was taking selfies and signing autographs for the fans. At the end of our conversation, we exchanged numbers and were adamant to keep in touch. During the GWS Giants first few seasons, I volunteered for their Membership and Fan Development Department. I sent Luke a message one day notifying him of my role within the club, and he suggested for me to head into the football department when I was next in.

Kel with the GWS Giants team

Growing up supporting an AFL team, I didn't need to second guess my reply and let him know I would come in next week. Fast forwarding a week... I couldn't believe my luck being able to just walk into the GWS Giants Football Department. Luke introduced me to the likes of Kevin Sheedy, Leon Cameron, Al McConnell, Lenny Hayes, Amon Buchanan, Chad Cornes, Dean Brogan, James McDonald, and Mark McVeigh. I was genuinely star struck. I then got to head into a meeting with Leon Cameron (GWS Giants Head Coach) and Luke Power. We discussed my life ambitions and some chat about where I wanted to be in a few years. Leon and Luke were so genuine and wanted the best for me and offered me a volunteering role within the football department with them. I was beyond excited and didn't have to think about a response. I said yes straight away without thinking about anything else. I couldn't believe how lucky I was. The following week, I woke up at 5 a.m. to catch public transport into Sydney Olympic Park. As I was walking into the football club, I couldn't believe who I was lucky enough to walk past, the likes of Jeremy Cameron, Toby Greene, Tom Scully, Will Hoskin-Elliott, Adam Treloar, Ryan Griffin, Stevie J, and Heath Shaw. Every single player who was on the list made time and effort to come introduce themselves to me, which honestly meant a lot, and I built a great rapport with all the players and saw them as "mates" instead of "footy players." Countless times a lot of the players went above and beyond for me. I had the likes of Will Hoskin-Elliott, Dylan Shiel, and Tom Scully drive me home to Western Sydney. I would find myself sitting down with the boys for lunch, and they wouldn't bat an eye lid at me.

During my time at GWS, Leon and Luke sat me down and discussed with me regarding the potential of telling my story to the playing group, and how I don't let my injuries get me down and how I've overcome adversity in my life. I drafted up a speech and

PowerPoint presentation and presented it to Leon, Luke, and some other staff members first. They were all taken back from my story and were thoroughly inspired. A few weeks later, after I had presented to Leon and Luke and the staff members, I had changed up a few things in the presentation and speech and was finding myself in front of the whole GWS Giants playing group. I looked around and took a deep breath. There were countless people in the room who I grew up "idolising." I was honestly star struck but continued with my story. After about 20 minutes, the presentation was finished and all the room applauded and they personally came up to me and told me how much I inspired them. I had the likes of Jeremy Cameron, Heath Shaw, Dylan Shiel, Tom Scully, Josh Kelly, and Adam Treloar all come up and personally tell me how much they appreciated me telling my story.

Our family friends are the Delezios. I grew up with Sophie and became a mentor to her, as every day we both suffer the consequences of living with injuries associated to our burns. Sophie went along to family camps for survivors run by the KIDS Foundation, and they were holding another camp at Collaroy, near Sydney. The Delezios were attending and kindly sponsored our family to join them. That is how I first became involved with the KIDS Foundation. On that camp, I was lucky enough to meet Susie, who was the founder of the organisation. I remember meeting Matt, who to this day is one of my closest mates, and I'm in regular contact with him.

Kel and Matt

I have been lucky enough to be a mentor to many young up and coming burn survivors through the KIDS Foundation. In 2012, I did my first KIDS Foundation Ambassador school visit. It was down in Cronulla where I was fortunate enough to partner with Matt and Reidy from Bondi Rescue. After the school assembly where Matt and Reidy and I had just spoken at, we were handing out KIDS merch and then all the school kids were wanting Matt's and my autograph. The school set up a table, and we were directed to grab a seat, sign the merch, and just engage with the school children. We thought it would be Reidy that the kids wanted autographs from, but a lot of the children were extremely excited and chuffed meeting Matt and I close up and personal. It was great to give back to the KIDS Foundation, and I'm glad the school children enjoyed it.

The following day, Matt and I went down to a fundraiser. We were introduced to the local member for the Sutherland area at the time, the Honourable Scott Morrison MP. We ended up sitting down at a local coffee shop with Mr. Morrison and Susie. We spoke about our injuries and how much the KIDS Foundation had done for us throughout our lives. Mr. Morrison was extremely appreciative. Sometime later, Susie approached Mr. Morrison about becoming an ambassador. He accepted, becoming our "Parliamentary Patron", and went on to become Prime Minister.

Lachie, Kel, Declan and Matt

I have attended several camps, and each time we get together, as well as experiencing new activities and exploring new places, we have time to share what we have been up to and usually have lots of stories to tell. One of the camps I attended a couple of years ago was in Rockingham WA. It was a camp mainly for teenagers. We flew from all over Australia into Perth and stayed at a school camp in Rockingham. Rockingham was chosen because the KIDS Foundation partners with HMAS Ballarat that is stationed at the Rockingham Base and CBA Rockingham had provided funding to hold the camp there. One of the activities was to travel to Fremantle and visit the prison. It was there I experienced something that was totally unexpected. I visualised my birth mum in prison for what she had done to me and had to leave. I sent a text message, which read, "Hey Susie, is it possible if we just have a chat?" We looked for a place to sit down, but there wasn't much around except a marketplace, so we opted for a coffee shop there. Once I had sat down with Susie, I remember bawling my eyes out. Being in a prison for the first time bought it all back. It was too much. I just personally couldn't be there, given my circumstances. I then went into details with Susie regarding how I sustained my burns and how the prison bought it all back. It was all just too much.

That evening back at the camp, we all designed a vision board, and Susie asked us to write down something we wished for or something we wanted to achieve, and she would try and help us make it happen. I believe everyone has had their wish granted, but I was waiting until my partner Bec, of five years, and I moved and got our own place. My wish was for a miniature dachshund, and on January 30, 2021, I got my wish. We picked up our puppy, Ollie. The KIDS Foundation, through the Carol Mayer Trust, bought Ollie for us. He is so, so cute, and we love him so much. He's so cheeky and gives the best puppy kisses and cuddles.

Kel and I walked down to find a quiet place to chat. We found a coffee shop at a close-by marketplace. Kel broke down and told me all about the incident that led to his burns. When the group had finished the prison tour, they joined us at the market. We all went into a stall that had gemstones, crystals and inspirational items. I asked each of the young people to select a stone. They all took this experience quite seriously, taking their time to choose a stone that resonated with them. One of the girls said when she picked up her crystal it gave her tingles in her hand and arm. Every crystal is supposed to have a different purpose, depending on what you are looking for. Listening to the reasons why they chose the stone they did was rewarding and really put positive intentions into their thinking, especially Kel's after what happened that day. Creating "Vision Boards" has become quite a regular activity at camp. Some take great pride and will spend hours constructing them. It is rewarding when life pans out the way they have visualised. Kel had planned to buy a puppy when he and Bec moved to their own place, and Ollie is now in their lives thanks to a very special person.

Many survivors of traumatic circumstances find great enjoyment giving back to others. Little did Carol know her legacy would continue, but not quite in the way she would have expected. In just days after her passing, a Trust was set up in her name. Some money went to a nurse that looked after Carol who was doing it though, so that she could have a special Christmas with her children. And, Kel got his puppy.

Kel, Bec and Ollie

Good friends are hard to find,
harder to leave
and impossible to forget.

- G. RANDOLF

"I've had so much enjoyment giving back, but there's still so much I want to do."

On the evening of February 3, 2000 around 10 p.m., a fire ripped through Carol Mayer's home and her life as she knew it was changed forever. She remembers eating tuna patties for dinner that night and dressing her son Zac, nearly two-years-old at the time, ready for bed. But, after that, Carol has no memories of the event that was the most defining day of her life. Shock had set in.

Carol suffered horrific burns to 85% of her body, and doctors didn't expect her to make it through the night, giving her a 50/50 chance of survival. A neighbour was able to push in a window screen and save Zac, unharmed, from the house. Carol was 33 at the time. She was placed in a coma in intensive care for six weeks. Although each day of the next few weeks were touch and go, she was a "fighter" and made it. It was four months before Carol got to look in a mirror and see her face. She remembers being absolutely devastated, and then she was to learn the doctors had to remove most of her fingers too.

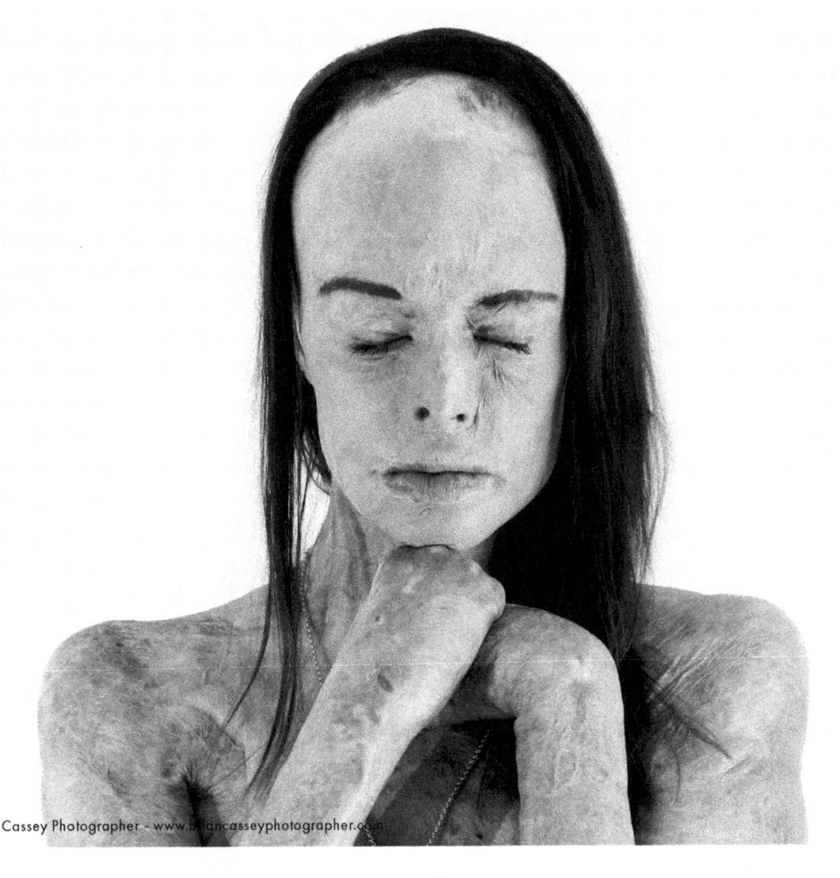

Brian Cassey Photographer - www.briancasseyphotographer.com

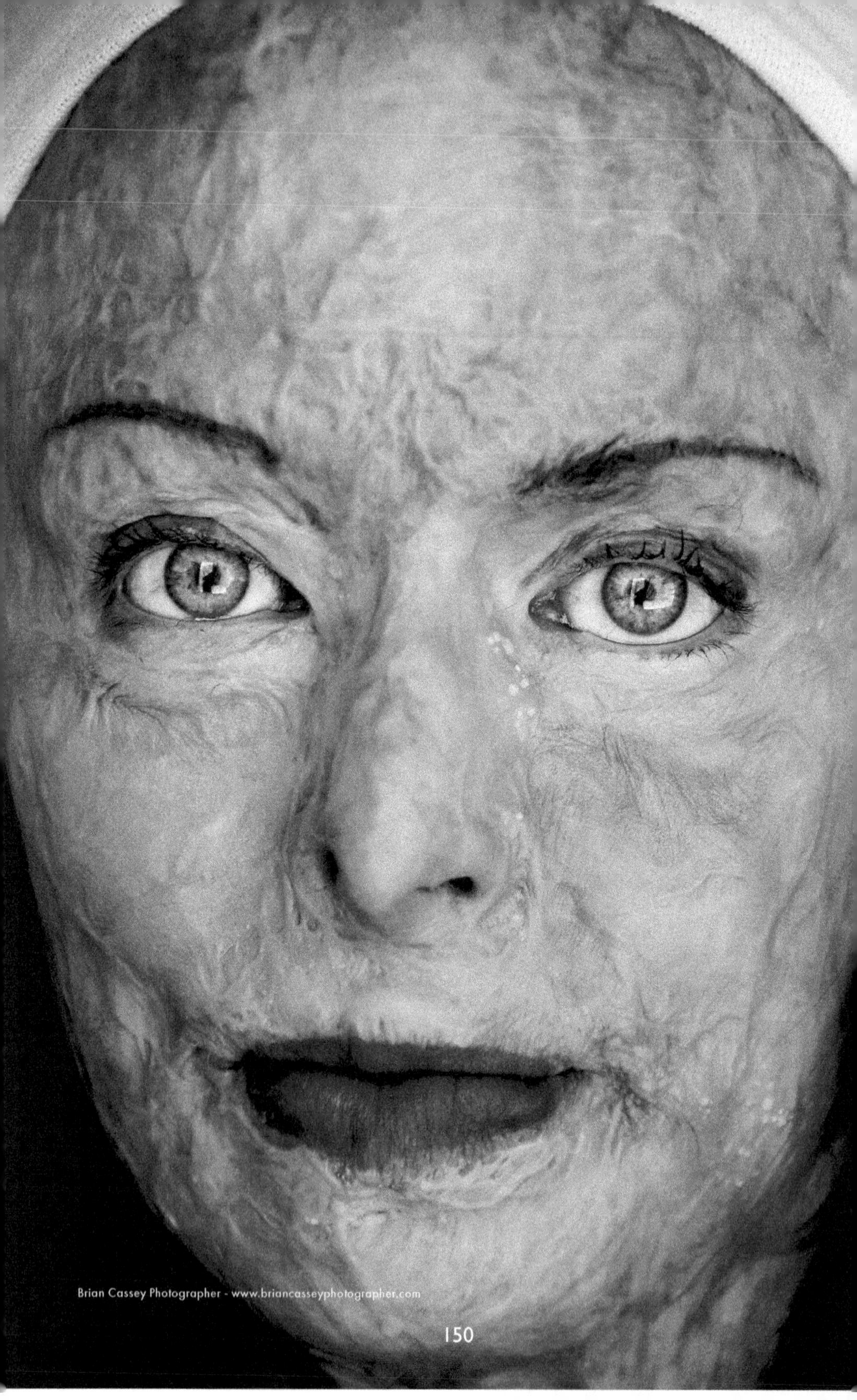
Brian Cassey Photographer - www.briancasseyphotographer.com

In August 2001, 18 months following the fire and after more than 100 painful operations, Carol was moved out of hospital into a house with her son Zac that had kindly been built by her local community. Her positive attitude and great sense of humour helped her to rebuild her life. There were stares walking through shopping centres. "Spiderwoman's here!" she would say as she laughed with the little kids.

It was around 2005 that Carol found the burn survivor community. Like many, she had thought she was the only one that had experienced what she had. She started meeting other survivors and began speaking about her story at events in front of more than 350 people. In 2017, Carol attended the World Burn Congress, where she got to meet her special friend Karen Jacques, who is one of the KIDS Foundation's true champs. In 2019, I was invited by Karen to speak at a retreat on the Sunshine Coast for adult survivors. It was there I got to meet Carol, and we instantly connected. She was eager to become a volunteer at our camps. I knew she would be an inspiration and great mentor to our young people.

Carol had posed for a well-known photographer, Brian Cassey. The Portrait, "The Skin I'm In," made it into the Portrait of Humanity 2020 shortlist. Another photo from the series was also finalist in the National Photographic Portrait Prize. Although Carol was not completely undressed, she felt a little nervous about having her photograph taken and exposing so much of her altered skin, but she said she trusted Cassey. When she saw the photos, she said it tells the picture as it is and was really happy with them. Carol said she didn't have any regrets and would do it all again, hoping the photos would empower other burns survivors, especially women.

Carol loved giving back and had great plans to help in many ways. She still had so much to do, but little did we know it would end too soon, and in this way. Here her brother, Russell reflects...

One of the many heart-to-hearts I had with Carol was about the unfinished business she had.

My darling sister Carol passed away on December 12, 2020 from a battle with stomach cancer. I wanted to honour her in a special way, a way somehow that would make her proud. She wanted to use the best of her ability to raise awareness for those suffering. She had so much to do in her mind, so much more for so many, as many as she could help. Carol knew her scars had pull, she knew those scars had influence, and she used them to the utmost of her ability to create awareness. She displayed her beautiful self the most openly she could to influence many. She put herself on the line!

This is how I believe Carol wants to be remembered. I remember not long after her death, feeling she was there helping me to decide what to do. I had a chill and goosebumps! She was right beside me. I knew my sister better than anyone - our hearts were one. I felt her spirit strongly with me, I felt her guiding me and telling me what to do. Carol had a special place in her heart for the KIDS Foundation, an organisation that we trust. Everyone responds to tragedies in different ways, but it was our choice not to create another charity, as it is a crowded space, but rather support this trusted organisation. KIDS Foundation is set up for donors to receive tax benefits, and donations are more likely to get quickly and efficiently to those in need. So, now we have the Carol Mayer Trust with 100% of donated funds used for burns and young trauma survivors and nurses that care for them, doing it tough.

At the time of Carol's death, there was a press frenzy going on as she had built quite a profile in the media. There were newspapers, TV stations, and radio stations contacting me. They said they could cut me some slack while we are mourning, but my sister Natalie and I said, "Bring it on." We must strike while the iron is hot. We got the message out that there was a trust being setup. It was going to be in Carol's honour. I had been working on this with two special ladies, Karen Jacques and Susie O'Neill.

Well, I sent my family and friends a message to tell them we had unfinished business. Together we could do this for Carol. Don't cry, don't let the grief of her death overcome you, instead celebrate one of the most amazing women to walk the earth. Let's pull some people out of hardship, let's make them smile. And high above us, Carol will smile. Please don't send flowers. Don't send anything. Let's honour her, and through the Carol Mayer Trust, right now. This is the cutting of the ribbon, the start of the race.

One of the many heart-to-hearts I had with Carol was about the unfinished business she had. A tear welled up in her eyes when she told me that. She told me that she is not afraid of dying, but she is so sad to be leaving her son Zac, not seeing him find a lady and having her grand kids, and also that she had unfinished business. We will continue her unfinished business and make it our business, continuing her legacy by giving to those in need - burns and trauma survivors, and the nurses that have supported them, that are doing it tough.

Brian Cassey Photographer - www.briancasseyphotographer.com

You are a very special person.
There is only one like
you in the whole world.
There's never been anyone
exactly like you before,
and there will never be again.
Only you.
And people can like you
exactly as you are.

- FRED ROGERS

Karen

From one burn survivor to another - Fly like the Phoenix.

Playing with fire is certainly not one of the smartest things I have done in my life. At the age of five back in 1968, I decided that I wanted to play with matches. I found a box of matches and snuck outside to our family garage to try and see what would happen if I struck the match. Little did I know that striking the match towards me instead of away from me would create years of pain, hell, and nightmares, not only for me but for my parents and siblings. I was wearing a nylon dress, it engulfed in flames within seconds. Back in the sixties, we were not taught to stop, drop, and roll, so I immediately started running into the house, not realising the flames had travelled straight up my back making the situation much worse. The smell of burning flesh is still very vivid to me 50 years later, and this is something that I will not forget ever. I was immediately transferred to Princess Margaret Hospital in Perth Burns Unit, and this is where I stayed for 12 months. I endured third degree full thickness burns to 70% of my little body, my mother giving me skin off her legs for my back as my body had no skin left to take. I remember screaming every time that the nurse would say "Bath Time," as I knew what was about to happen - debriding the dead skin so the new skin could come through. Debriding is like getting a cheese grater and scraping it on your skin. There were no memory drugs given back in the 60s, or pain killers for that matter, but I learned to just suck it up, as no matter how much I screamed or begged the nurses not to put me into the bath, it had to be done. I believe today they do this procedure while the patient is asleep or given Medazalline, which is a memory drug. The photos below were taken about three years after my burn. Most of my primary school was done in hospital as I always had lengthy stays after each surgery.

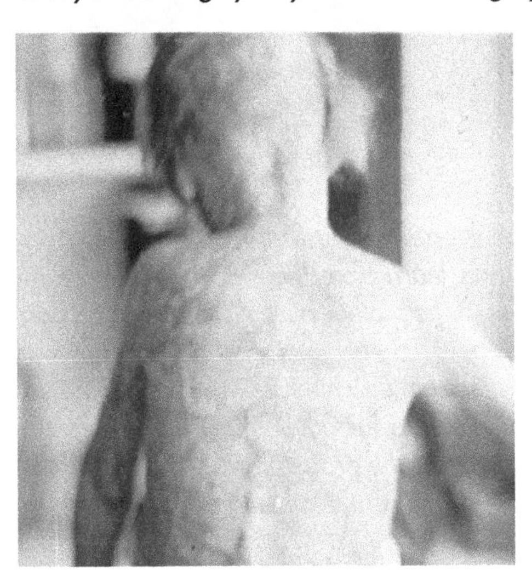

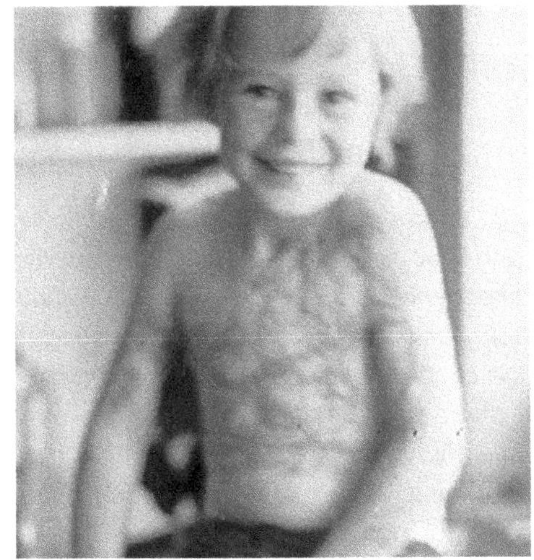

After many years of countless surgeries, skin grafts, and hospital visits, I finally started high school. High school was like torture for me. Attending a Catholic School in Perth, my parents thought that this was the best for me as they thought that I would not be teased. How wrong were they. I was tortured on a daily basis being called names like Towering Inferno, Baldie (as I lost a lot of my own hair), and many other names. I also did have some beautiful school friends, one including my now husband Paul. As soon as I could finish high school, which was in year 10, I got a job at Kentucky Fried Chicken. I had not met anyone else that had been burnt, so I felt very isolated through my primary and high school years. No one understood what I went through and the pain that I still endured years after my burn.

I moved out of home at the age of 16 and shared a unit with my friend Alison, whom I knew from the age of five. At the age of 18, I joined the Australian Army. My grandad was in the Army, and I wanted to follow in his footsteps. I was initially refused entry into the Army as they said that my burns would stop me doing the activities required to be a soldier, but after much determination and a visit to the dermatologist, I was finally cleared and enlisted and served 11 years in the Army. While in the Army, I met my first husband and had two beautiful daughters, Hayley and Emma. Initially I was told that having children would not be easy as my skin would not stretch. I proved them wrong again, although my skin did have several break downs, it did not have any elasticity where I was burnt.

2019 Burn Survivors Retreat

At the age of 30, I discovered that there was support in Australia for burn survivors, and I wanted to meet other burn survivors and learn from them and also share my experiences. This is where I began volunteering to help other burn victims become burn survivors. I discovered the KIDS Foundation about 15 years ago but never really had the courage to approach them. I did a lot of research into the KIDS Foundation before I offered my services to them in a way of mentorship for other burn survivors. I had attended a few KIDS camps and was blown away by the professionalism and kindness that this charity offered. The admiration from families and other burn survivors was very obvious to me.

I am now 57 years of age and have seven grandchildren, and I live a very healthy and beautiful life married to my childhood sweetheart Paul. It took me a lot of years not to wear long sleeves and cover up, and this is due to meeting other burn survivors and realising that it is only my skin that was burnt, not my heart, not my soul, and if people don't like to look at my scars, then I do not care anymore as this is their problem not mine.

The KIDS Foundation brings families and burn survivors together by holding camps all around Australia. These camps are so important not only to the burn survivor, but also the families. I have seen first-hand what a difference these camps make especially to the kids. It is so important to burn survivors and their families to be able to come together and chat about each person's experiences. I have met some amazing and beautiful people through the KIDS Foundation that will be friends for life. I cannot recommend the KIDS Foundation highly enough and would encourage any burn or injury survivor to reach out to the KIDS Foundation, as there is support there for you, and who knows, you may even make a few friends.

I consider myself very blessed, although most of my body is scarred and I overheat frequently. My scars tell a story. A story that I survived a very terrible accident, but I hold my head up high, and I am grateful for every day that I am alive. So, if you have a serious injury or are a burn survivor, never give up. There is always that light at the end of the tunnel, and remember, there is support out there. It does get easier day by day, and just take one step at a time, one day at a time, and be happy to be alive.

Make the most of what you have and don't focus on the negatives.

Karen has not let her injuries stop her from activities most would find challenging. Karen rode 600km with me on a KIDS ride, volunteers at camps and partcipates in all activities. In 2021, Karen joins me in Adventure All Stars Charity Global TV. She channels her energy into raising funds and awareness for the KIDS Foundation, supporting fellow survivors along the way. Karen is a special person we love dearly.

Brett, Declan, Don, Karen, John, Susie, Brad, Annie, Craig, Annie, Scott and Sue

You dream. You plan. You reach.
There will be obstacles.
There will be doubters.
There will be mistakes.
But with hard work,
with belief, with confidence
and trust in yourself
and those around you,
there are no limits.

- MICHAEL PHELPS

CHAPTER SIX

Not being able to do enough

The thing I don't cope with the most is not being able to do more for the courageous, inspirational people one could ever meet.

People will often ask, "How do you cope emotionally?" When I first ran the camps, I found it would take about a month to get over some of the visible injuries I had witnessed and stories heard at a camp. At the time, I didn't take staff with me or engage friends. Most of the team were made up of volunteers. But a few years on, I needed a nurse to accompany us on the camp due to the number of children that needed delicate dressing changes and administration of medicines, so I invited my very dear, beautiful friend Beth Bromley.

Beth had the saddest circumstances happen in her life. She knew too well the trauma a tragic circumstance can bring, losing her first husband in a work accident, where he was electrocuted in the home he was working in. She had shared a special surprise with her husband that day, that they were expecting their second baby. Sadly, Beth lost her baby due to the trauma caused through losing her husband. And, if that wasn't enough for one person to endure, later in life Beth lost her partner and soulmate Phil through cancer and is now fighting that same disease herself. To this day, Beth is the longest serving and most loyal of camp volunteers, known as the comforter and grandmother of the team.

When we return home from camps and catch up for our regular social occasions, we chat about our experience at the previous camp. Beth has been my "sounding board," the go-to therapy I have needed for over 28 years. Someone to chat with that knew exactly what I was talking about and feeling. That is one of the most effective practises that we have introduced into camps. We put systems in place to ensure we have a support person for each volunteer at camp, either someone from their workplace or friendship circle, to ensure they are not alone.

It can be quite stressful at times and even trigger responses relating to personal experiences, but the thing I don't cope with the most is not being able to do more. Sometimes I just want to take these children home, and that nearly happened on several occasions until Brett reminded me that we had four children of our own who would be impacted. My mum would often say that Brett was my handbrake, and she was right, as I would probably have an orphanage of children by now if that wasn't the case. I must admit Brett has been extremely tolerant of my passion for the Foundation. The only time he said it nearly broke him was the time we sold our home and moved to our rental property to be able to keep the Foundation going.

Fortunately, Brett has a successful plumbing business and we soon got back on our feet. Over the years, he has donated a lot of time and money to support the Foundation. Our children have been heavily involved also, but they have their own lives and careers. The things that I wished for most from my children were that they shared the same values of trust, loyalty, and kindness and were just good caring individuals, and that they are. At times, they have joined me on our recovery camps and been moved by the young people they have met. Kate, now a mum and primary teacher, attended a camp we held in Queensland. At the time, she was 12 years old and wrote an essay for a school project about a young girl whose story touched her heart.

PREVENTION
- RECOVERY
FROM INJURY
& BURNS
K·I·D·S
PREVENTION
-RECOVERY
FROM INJURY
& BURNS
K·I·D·S
FOUNDATION

How ironic that our family
should be a safe haven.
Our parents and siblings
are supposed to love us,
accept us, and care for us.
They should protect us
and support us.
Sometimes, our home is where
we find the deepest heartaches.

- DANA ARCURI

Jean

A house fire, abuse and a car accident is more than one little person should of have had to endure.

By Kate O'Neill (2002)...

Last year I went to a burns camp. I've been to a few burns' camps - there are about two or three camps a year. At the camps, you do lots of activities like swimming, canoeing, snorkelling, fishing, high ropes courses, and lots more. Water activities are very important activities at a burns camp because survivors are often afraid of water. Some survivors are injured from boiling water and others have to have very painful baths to remove the dead skin. Some survivors are so scared of water that they don't have baths and showers. The camps are held in places where they can have fun in water and teach them that water is not bad, then they are not so scared to have baths and showers. Some of the camps are family camps because it is not only the burns survivors that need hope. After a burns accident, family members suffer too. People that have been burnt come to the camps to meet other survivors and to have fun. Sometimes when they walk down the street or go somewhere, people stare and point. At the camps, people who are burnt meet other people that have been burnt, and they feel like they are normal again.

Last year in November, we went to Brisbane for a burns camp, and one of the activities was at the South Gate swimming pool where we had a bit of free time. One of the burns survivors was swimming in the pool where he met a girl the same age as he was. She looked like she was badly burnt. She asked him, "Who are you here with?" He said, "I'm on a burns camp, and I'm from Victoria". He asked her name, she replied "I'm Jean". Then he introduced her to all of us, and we invited her to have lunch. Nick Green (rowing champion) from the Oarsome Foursome was our group leader and said Jean could join into our group activities.

Later we found out that Jean was in a house fire, and she lost her eight-year-old brother and her four-year-old twin sisters in the fire. Her mother left home, her family separated, and Jean went to live with her father. Jean's dad had to go away for a little bit to work, so she stayed with her uncle. Jean got abused by her uncle and was not treated very well, so she went back with her dad. Jean's dad began a relationship with a lady. She was having trouble accepting it, so she ran away from home. Jean had been living in a woman's refuge centre for the last six months.

We had lunch in a big restaurant and Jean came with us. When we got to the airport and were getting ready to leave, Jean was still with us, sitting with our group and Nick.

Mum asked Nick why Jean was still with us, and he said she didn't want to go back. Jean asked my mum if she could come back with us, but there were not enough plane tickets. So, Mum said she would contact her the next day and see what she could do. The next day, Mum did ring and found out she had been living in a women's refuge. That is why she didn't want to go home, she had no home. A few months later, Mum arranged for Jean to come down to the next burns camp, which was held in Ballarat. When she arrived, she didn't have many clothes and her toes were hanging out of the end of her sandshoes. Mum went and bought some new clothes and shoes. They were Nike runners. She was so happy she hugged Mum and cried happy tears. After the camp, she wanted to stay, and so Mum arranged for her to go and live with another family. She went to school and was doing year 11 when her dad asked if she would go back to Brisbane to live with him again.

Jean took her two pet kittens back to Brisbane with her. She rang Mum every week to talk to her and let her know how she was going and that she was happy. One day, Mum got a phone call from the Government department to say Jean had died in a car accident. On the June 9, Jean and her dad were in a car crash, and Jean had very bad head injuries. She later died on June 11. The lady from the Government told us how much she loved us and that we had given her the best time of her life. Mum was really sad, but that made her smile.

Jean was a really nice person; she would come up to you and give you a big hug. Everyone loved her and couldn't wait to see her at the next camp. We will really miss her.

Chris Lee with Jean, Giselle and Bianca

Camp Phoenix Tangalooma 2013

The only person
you are destined to
become is the person
you decide to be

- RALPH WALDO EMERSON

Ryan

Just three days before Christmas, so badly burnt, he was unrecognisable and was mistaken for his brother.

Over the years, we have been welcomed into the lives of families that have had endured unimaginable tragedies, where children have died, and others have survived. On this occasion, it was a car crash in NSW that took the life of three young children. Ryan survived, but was so badly burnt he was mistaken for his brother Dylan.

It was just three days before Christmas and the family were looking forward to spending the Christmas holidays with their loved ones and the big family gathering that had been planned at their grandmother's place. The car was packed with the presents, along with their luggage, and they headed off in the early hours of the morning. They did it that way so their four young children could sleep through most of the trip. There were two-year-old twins, Ryan and Emily, Dylan three years old, and seven-year-old Ashley. Sadly, things didn't go as planned. At around 8:10 a.m. on December 22,1994, along the New England Highway near Uralla NSW, there was a head-on collision between two cars. Their family van was one of them. It incinerated on impact. The accident tragically claimed the lives of the driver of the other vehicle and the lives of three of the children, Ashley, Dylan, and Emily. Ryan, his dad, and mum survived, but were in a critical condition suffering from horrific burns and multiple injuries. The footage of the wreckage on the news they later shared with me was devastating. How anyone survived was beyond belief.

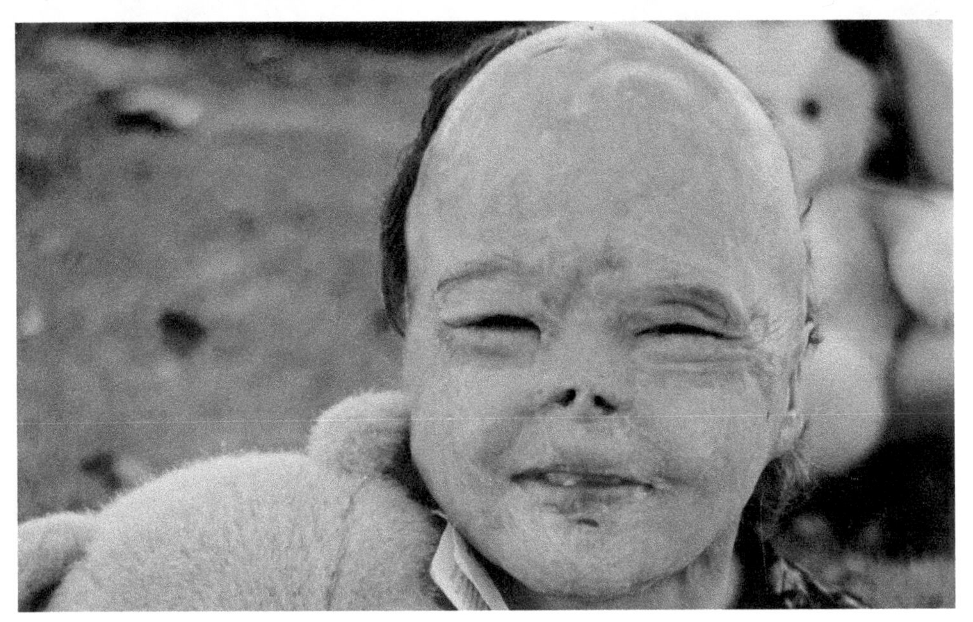

The upset and traumatised police officers were given the duty of taking the devastating news to grandparents, who were at home expecting the family to arrive for Christmas. That was the day that changed the whole extended family's lives, in the most unimaginable way. The officers drove the grandparents to the Armidale Hospital, where the survivors had been taken. Along the way, the officers had to prepare them for what they were about to witness. The survivors had suffered horrific injuries, and they were not expected to live. The grandparents were able to briefly see them before air ambulances flew them to better equipped hospitals in Sydney. Stretchered onto the planes on life-support, they were transported to three different hospitals to give them the best chance of survival. Ryan's dad had to have both legs amputated and suffered horrific burns. Lisa, Ryan's mum, suffered full thickness burns to 80% of her body. The surviving child who was thought to be Dylan, was actually one of the twins, Ryan. Ryan, aged just two, the twin brother of Emily, had survived but suffered a broken leg and burns to 40% of his body. He had full thickness burns to his face and head, losing most of his hair, as well as the amputation of all his fingers and thumbs.

The fact that the surviving family members were being treated in three different hospitals meant it was to be some time before they were able to hold each other in their arms. The family members rallied around to make sure someone was there for each of them. Having a supportive family around can be one of the greatest successors for healing. The parents had their own physical healing to do, but the emotional suffering was inconceivable. For a parent to endure losing one child is traumatic, but to lose three children is unimaginable. A few years on, some of their pain was eased with the arrival of two more beautiful children. First the arrival of Tori and then Darcy. They brought so much happiness into their shattered lives.

Ryan with Casey Barnes

The thing that sticks in my head most about Ryan is his ability to tie shoelaces with no fingers. His injuries left him with no fingers and thumbs. The very clever surgeons removed a toe from his foot and attached it to his hand to make a thumb that allowed him to go on and tackle things equally as capable as someone with five fingers on each hand. He was a true inspiration to the younger children. The children would watch Ryan in amazement and then would say, "If Ryan can do it so can I."

Susie, Paul Harragon and Ryan

At the camps, he was the first person to raise his hand to help and was never one to buckle at hard work. He attempted every activity that was thrown at him and was a natural at it, like the time we taught him to water ski and he got up first go. Ryan made the Parramatta Eales Junior Development Squad and featured on the NSW Footy Show. At one of the camps, I asked the children who their idlos were and attempted to arrange for the celebrities they selected to come to a special day organised at Australia Zoo. Ryan's idlo was Paul Harragon from the Newcastle Knights, nicknamed the Chief, Chief Harragon. He captained the team to win their first ever ARL premiership (now the NRL—National Rugby League) in 1997 and represented Australia in a senior men's international football competitions. I made contact with Paul, and he accepted, bringing along his film crew. A week later, we were featured on the Footy Show, which was a thrill for all the children. They themselves felt like celebrities.

It is so rewarding to speak with the families and hear how well they are doing. Recently I had a chat with Lisa, and she shared that Ryan is now 28 and a proud dad to Carter. He is getting to live his dream, which was always to drive monster trucks. Ryan has just secured a job driving the big trucks in the mines.

It's true.
Each one of us is special.
That's because of
who we are inside.

- FRED ROGERS

"Will Santa think I'm yucky?"

Just before Christmas on December 4, 2007, mother of two boisterous young boys, Dee, grabbed the opportunity to take a quick shower while her boys were outside playing. Dee remembers...

Paul (the boy's dad) had headed off to work and the boys were playing in the backyard, so I thought I would grab the opportunity to take a quick shower. Suddenly I could smell smoke and it was coming from the kids' bedroom. I ran to the room through the door, but I couldn't see a thing. The smoke was that thick it was billowing out. I could hear Rhys crying, and I frantically felt my way through the smoke to find him. I picked him up and ran out of the house. His face was covered in ash, but he seemed okay, so I went back to find Brock. It was so hot in the room that I couldn't breathe. I searched for him amongst the thick smoke and when I found him, he was huddled underneath the cot. I grabbed him and ran as fast as I could back out to where Rhys was. Brock was alive but was badly burnt, his hair singed, and face was all blotchy. I quickly ran with the boys to Dianne's house, my next door neighbour. When she saw us, she took us to her bathroom and into the shower to run cold water over us. As the water ran over Brock, his hair washed off his head and his little body was covered in blisters. Dianne rang for an ambulance and called Paul to tell him what had happened. The ambulance arrived and took us to the local hospital where Paul was waiting anxiously for us to arrive. Brock's burns were so severe he had to be flown to the Royal Children's Hospital (RCH) and placed in an induced coma. Paul accompanied Brock in the helicopter and his mum took charge of Rhys. Unbeknown to me, I had also suffered 25% burns to my face, arms, back, and knees. The shock of the situation and panic to save the boys had left me numb. I couldn't feel any pain. I was taken to the Caulfield Hospital and also put into an induced coma to allow my body to heal.

I woke four days later to Paul telling me Brock was alive. The next day I was taken to the ICU. I had no idea what I was about to walk into. He had suffered 45% full thickness burns and was laying there covered from head to toe, swathed in wadding and bandages, with just his toes exposed. He had a bunch of tubes poking out everywhere. All I could do was carefully stroke his toes and tell him we were there and how much we loved him. It was so hard to leave him and go back to hospital where I was being treated. I cried all the way back; it would be another agonising week before I would get to see Brock again. During this whole time, his little body was fighting to stay alive. He fought pneumonia and a severe infection that threatened the loss of his fingers and potentially his arms. The doctors were concerned that he was not going to survive. What was to follow next was several weeks of sheer hell - 50 skin graft operations.

When I had been released from hospital, I didn't want to leave his side, reading his favourite book Guess How Much I Love You over and over again. That is one Christmas that we will never forget. It was horrible. Brock was that sick and weak, he didn't have the strength to open his gifts. The police said how the fire started was a mystery. There was very little that remained of the house, actually nothing at all. The fact that it was an old wooden house meant that it burnt very quickly, within minutes. But that was the least of my worries. Even though we lost everything materialistic, it didn't matter. As long as we had our two boys, that is all that mattered.

We sat beside Brock's bed waiting for him to open his eyes. Eventually he did a few weeks later. When he woke, we tried to explain to him that he was very sick. He tried to talk, but the tracheal tube in his throat made it impossible. He looked at us with those innocent, wide eyes as they filled with tears. I reassured him, "Mama is here." It was after weeks of speech therapy that one day he whispered, "Mama." It was the happiest day of my life. Brock eventually came home after five months in hospital. At first Rhys was too scared to go near him. We had to take it slowly and explain that although he looked different, it was the same Brocky. As the bandages came off, Rhys became more comfortable being around him. But then there was the mocking from other children when we were out. As if he hadn't been through enough without people starring and being insensitive to his appearance and what he had been through.

Then in August we were contacted by the KIDS Foundation. One of their programs was the Burn Survivors' Network. There were lots of children that had been badly burnt like Brock. Until then, we hadn't met any other children with injuries similar to Brock's. We no longer felt alone. It was comforting to speak with other families that had been through what we had. It gave us hope everything was going to be okay. From then on, Brock got stronger every day. It was coming up to Christmas nearly a year from that tragic day when we took a trip to the local shopping centre to meet Santa. As we walked toward him, Brock asked, "Will Santa think I'm yucky?" and then went up to him and asked, "Can I sit on your lap?" "Sure thing, kiddo," he replied. I madly took photos thinking how special that Christmas was going to be. Brock may be scarred for life, but that has not dented his fighting spirit.

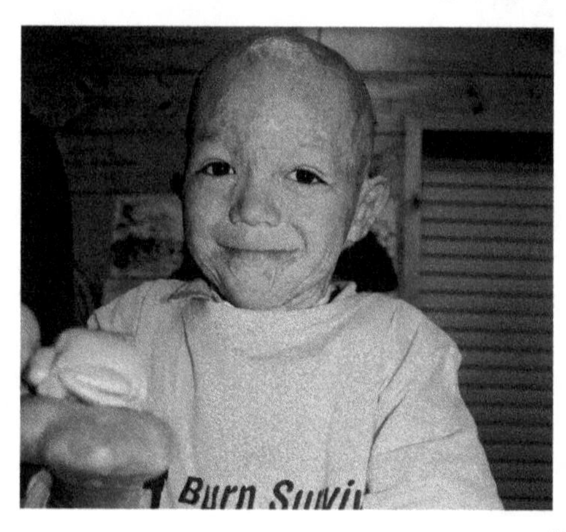

Brock with his mum Dee

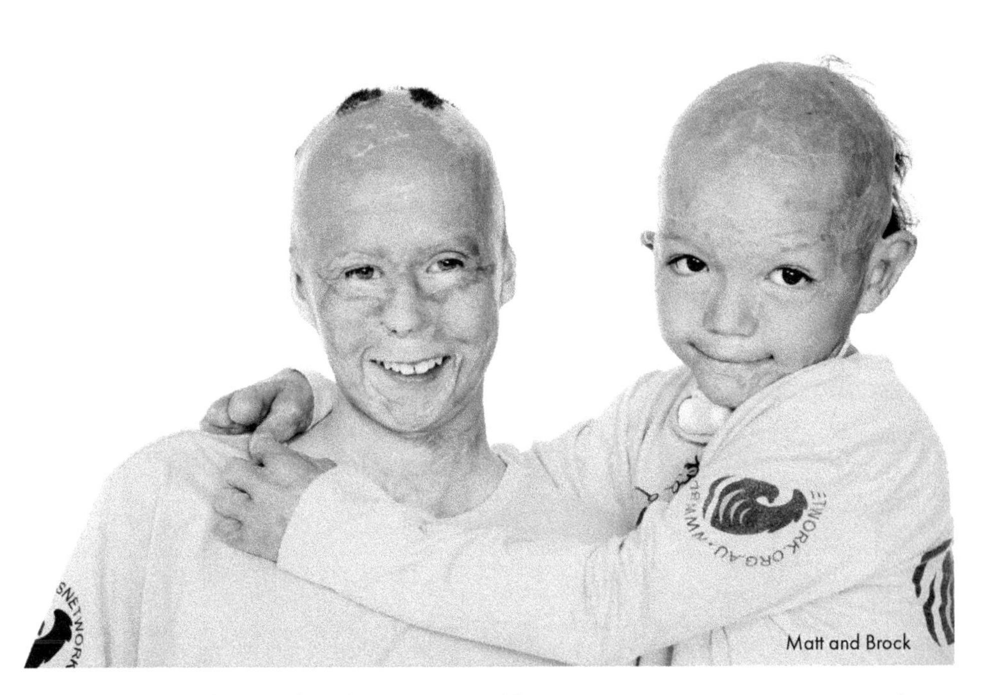

Matt and Brock

Today Brock is a happy, healthy, 17-year-old young man. We give KIDS Foundation full credit for helping us give Brock back his self-confidence and outgoing personality. He loves camps and has made some great friends. A lot of the kids we met in 2008 have gone on to become mentors to Brock and the other children. It's this support group and network that we as a family have come to rely on and cherish.

Brock was a real cutey, a boisterous four-year-old when he came to his first camp. Everyone loved his energy, especially our generous sponsor Darren from Giant Bikes. Darren asked if there were any children that needed a bike for Christmas. I was sure Brock and Rhys would welcome a bike considering they had lost everything in the fire the Christmas before. We took the boys to the Giant Head Office a few days before Christmas, and they were overwhelmed. Every year thereafter, Darren would take the family to breakfast just before Christmas and present them with a well thought out gift. Well so he thought. Darren was blessed with two girls, three now, so shopping for the boys was a novelty. One Christmas, he bought Nerf Guns and told them to wait to open the present until they got to the Giant store that was close by. They did love their presents, more than anything, but the store owner certainly did not. They let the bullets fly everywhere; the staff were picking them out of bike wheels and bits for days.

Over the years, there have been some of the most inspirational children that despite their horrific circumstances see their experience with fire as creating a positive life path that would have been very different had the event that day not happened. They are the sort of children that are able to take emotional responsibility of their situation by being open and accepting of themselves, others, and circumstances that come into their everyday life.

You don't have to live forever,
you just have to live.

– NATALIE BABBITT

Kane

Cheeky Kane, known to the KIDS family as the funniest kid with the biggest heart. His wit, magic tricks and fantastic sense of humour made us laugh, kept us entertained and showed us a different way to manage life's challenges.

The first time we met Kane was at Camp Phoenix, at Tangalooma on Moreton Island in 2013. He had been buddied up with John Minto, a volunteer with two sons of his own around the same age. We had been given a heads up that Kane would probably give his buddy 'a run for their money' as the saying goes, and we thought John would have the experience to manage him. As it turned out he did, and they became best buddies.

Kane would innocently do things at the most unexpected moments. There was a time he wandered into a volunteer briefing session with a flapping fish, casually announcing that he had just caught it off the pier on Moreton Island. Everyone went into a frenzy and then hysterics at the sight before them. At another camp in Noosa he decided to challenge us in true 'Kane style'. We had a little chat, as we often did, and I told him how much I loved his good self and how I could really do with a helper and could he be that person. His behaviour for the remainder of the camp was impeccable. Kristy (Kane's foster mother) rang me the following week and said, "whatever you said to him in that little chat needs to be bottled". His teachers could not believe the Kane that had turned up at school the following week.

Kane and Susie

John Minto and Kane

Kane continued the role of 'helper' at every camp, initiating assistance whenever he saw it was needed. He took a particular liking to photography at camp, and it was not unusual to find him with a camera in hand, running around assisting the designated camp photographer to capture some great images. We believed in him, and he excelled. Kane loved life, lived it to the fullest without hesitation and pushed the boundaries to the limit. Kane went through more challenges in life than any child deserves, but he just got on with it and fought hard to overcome his battles.

On Thursday, May 27, 2021 along with another teenager Kane was involved in a motorcycle accident in Tasmania. The boys were riding a trail bike that crashed with a motor vehicle throwing them from the bike. Both received significant injuries and were transported to hospital in a critical condition.

It was the most heartbreaking news when we heard that Kane had passed away after having his life support turned off. When told of his passing, many remembered the funny antics and loveable boy they had met and tributes flowed on social media, capturing his uniqueness - "Kane lived every moment and made the most of it; "Definitely his own character with one of the biggest hearts I am proud to say I knew", "He lived life to the fullest and had a heart of gold, his memory will live on with us and he has left such an impact on everyone." Everyone that knew Kane loved him, he was so special to so many. We miss seeing him, talking to him, and spending time with him at camp. He'll live forever in the hearts of those who loved him and all in the KIDS family.

Kristy tells his story - Kane Matthew Leary March 12, 2004 - May 30, 2021

Kane was born into a big family on 12th of March 2004 in Launceston. He had eight brothers and sisters, Christie-lee, Zane, Amy, Gilbert, Tyson, Judith, Kaleb and Yassie. Their dad Mathew sadly passed away when he was only 5 years old. Kane always wished he had more time with his dad and got to do all the things dads and sons do. But he loved his Mum Melissa unconditionally, and everyone knew she was the most important person in the world to him. Kane was known as his Mum's little protector, often running out the door telling Melissa to stay inside, like she was a child. He was definitely the man of the house. Kane had a love for music, the outdoors, push bikes, parties, swimming, fishing, motorbikes, animals and wildlife, especially reptiles. But there is nothing he loved more than his family.

You would have thought Tyson and Kane were twins, they had a bond like no other. Throughout life they were inseparable, always out on adventures, catching lizards and yabbies or any other creature they could find. One day Kane was playing under their house with his brother when they came across a lighter, he was just four years old at the time. Their relentless flicking of the button caused the flame to ignite, catching fire to Kane's clothes. This was the beginning of a long road to a traumatic recovery. Kane had sustained 47% burns to his little body and was not expected to live. The area's that were most affected on Kane's body were his face, neck, and upper body. He spent one year in Melbourne at the Royal Children's Hospital, having numerous surgeries and painful procedures to improve his movement and mobility. However, the barriers that come from this type of injury were no barriers for Kane. He just dealt with what he had and fought through all the pain, living life to the fullest. Always remaining happy, humble and strong.

As Kane grew older his aftercare and surgeries were then performed in the burns Unit at the Royal Hobart Hospital until moving to Queensland with his sister Amy to live with me. Kane had gained an extended family in myself, Corey, Rick, Trent, Zac, Shane, Jess and Steph. In Queensland, Professor Kimble took over Kane's burn management. Kane thought he was amazing as he was able to bring his pain management under control. He certainly kept the nurses on their toes though, entertaining them and preventing them from getting bored in the middle of the night and using the hospital phones to prank call as many people as he could. Kane certainly left a lasting impression on all the hospital staff and patients.

We lived on the Gold Coast for two years experiencing so many things from theme parks, footy, jet skiing and again creating so many other friendship groups. When Kane turned 14 he decided to move back to Tasmania to be where his heart was, with his mum and family, this is where he remained until his accident. We will miss him terribly and the laughter he brought into our lives.

Turn your scars into stars.

– ROBERT SCHULLER

Brittney

"Even in the hardest and darkest moments of our lives, we all have the strength to turn our scars into stars."

Finding a box of matches in the backyard of a house that Brittney's family had just moved into changed their life forever. As a little girl, she would ask her Mum, "When are the scars and all of this going to go away forever?" But they never will. Brittney will be recovering from her burns for the rest of her life. She credits her recovery to, as she puts it, "the best and most caring family in the world, my mum, dad, brother, and grandparents.

It is not just me who has to deal with my burns; it is my whole family. The other reason that gave me hope was the great support network we found that has helped me and my family get through the emotional, painful, and traumatic recovery periods. The organisation is the KIDS Foundation. I would not be the person I am today if it weren't for the KIDS Foundation. I feel that I have been given a gift and that gift is to help others recover from and prevent injuries like mine from happening. I tell others that I am not a victim, I am a survivor, a BURN SURVIVOR."

Susie and Brittney

On September 2, 1998, Brittney's family's world changed with just one strike of a match. Brittney was four years old at the time. It was around lunch time when she found a box of matches, took one out, struck it, and within seconds, flames had engulfed her body. Brittney's hair caught on fire, and her body and mind were consumed with the most unbearable pain. She was quickly thrown under an outside running tap. The pressure of the water ripped burnt remains of her dress away, and then her skin followed with it. Brittney's burns were so deep in some places the bone was exposed. She had received 40% full thickness burns to her body. What followed was nine months in hospital, hours of surgery, 83 skin grafts, synthetic skin implants, and years of rehabilitation. That became her life, in and out of school, to attend follow up appointments, more grafts, and hospitalisations. Due to infection risks at times, Brittney was hidden from family and friends. Growing up, "different" to everyone else so she thought, was challenging, dealing with the eyes that stare, the whispering voices, and the ones that just didn't want to acknowledge her. She said at times it was easier for her to accept the negative and hurtful comments and see herself as different rather than to try and defend it.

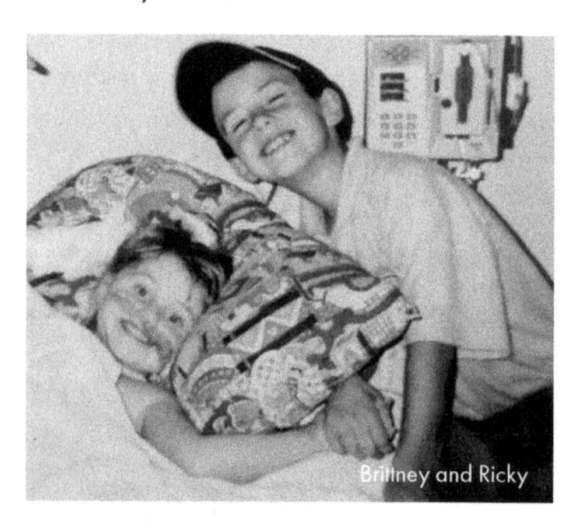

Brittney and Ricky

Brittney

In 2004, the family was on their way to a KIDS Foundation burn survivors camp in NSW. They stopped to take a rest at the seaside town of Nambucca Heads and took a walk along the break wall. The break wall was lined with hundreds of painted rocks. There were some really beautiful ones that had names and pictures, some in memory of lost loved ones. Brittney came across one rock towards the end of the wall, painted with a lime green top and these words written on it: "Turn your scars into stars." Brittney resonated with these words and took a photo, which she brought along to camp. At each camp, we allow time to reflect on our favourite part of the week. During the session, Brittney painted a picture of the ocean with the rock and the words, "Turn your scars into stars," and gave it to me as a gift. From that day, these words became a motto and a huge part of the KIDS Foundation philosophy. It also became Brittney's everyday mantra and a reminder to look at things differently, her world in a new light. For many years, Brittney became an inspiration for younger survivors and took on mentor and leadership roles as she grew older. She became a wonderful public speaker, talking at KIDS Foundation functions and sharing her story to inspire others. Brittney would say, "My skin doesn't phase me, nor do I let people's opinions of it phase me either. I've now grown to see our skin as a canvas throughout our lives, collecting detailed pieces of unique art for a story to come together after many years. Sure, we may have a few imperfections on the base to start off with, a couple of brush marks that appear throughout, but at the end of the day, no two people have a single mark that is the same, and to me that is something spectacular and beautiful. Some people would call my experience 'tragic.' I see it instead as a life-changing opportunity."

From these experiences that begin tragically, many survivors shape their future and find their life passion. Brittney graduated from University with a Bachelor of Nursing and ended up in the children's hospital that once cared for her. She even got to work alongside other nurses and doctors who were there for her and her family, supporting them through the hardest days of their recovery. To this day, Brittney continues to practice the "turn your scars into stars" mantra, sharing it to influence, guide, heal, and show others. She says "that even in the hardest and darkest moments of our lives, we all have the strength to 'turn our scars into stars.'"

Brittney has found the love of her life and is soon to be married. She is an inspiration to the young girls who wonder if they will ever find someone that will accept their scars and see them as perfect, just the way they are, like Jacob sees Brittney.

Jacob and I met while both travelling Vietnam back in 2017. After locking eyes on multiple occasions through the streets of the ancient town in Hoi An. I finally got a chance to speak with this stranger who I couldn't get out of my mind and from that day on we haven't stopped speaking. On November 20, 2021, exactly 4 years to the day we met in Vietnam, Jacob and I will be married at Jacob's family farm in Ganmain, NSW. I get to marry the most perfect person for me. A man who challenges me and inspires me daily. A man who never looked twice at what was on the outside but encouraged me more to show the world the person I am. Jacob and I live in Wagga Wagga, NSW. While I work full time as a Registered Nurse at the local hospital, Jacob runs Cobrapparel our custom headwear and apparel business full time.

Brittney and Jacob

Champions keep playing
until they get it right.

– BILLIE JEAN KING

The return of a champion.

On October 12, 2002, while on an end of football season trip in Bali with my North Melbourne teammate, Mick Martyn, the unimaginable occurred - a terrorist attack in Kuta. The attack focused on two bars in Kuta, Paddy's Bar and the Sari Club. Unfortunately, Mick and I and two other friends from Perth, Peter Hughes and Gary Nash, were in Paddy's Bar. Little to our knowledge, at that very moment, a suicide bomber was five metres from where we were standing and detonated a bomb. Within minutes of this blast, a car bomb was detonated only 25 members up the road out the front of the Sari Club.

Unfortunately, 202 people were killed in this attack including 88 Australians. The four of us were among the lucky ones to survive albeit suffering varying levels of injuries. Mine were life-threatening, suffering 50% burns and multiple shrapnel wounds. I was operated on in the Sanglah Hospital in Denpasar in the early hours of Sunday morning before finally being evacuated to Australia. My journey home to Melbourne was via Darwin, where I received the most amazing care before being flown to Melbourne. My destination in Melbourne would be the Alfred Hospital. Words cannot describe my gratitude to the Alfred and their amazing staff. On arrival at the Alfred Hospital, I was rushed straight to ICU where emergency surgery was performed, which included numerous skin grafts. Within 48 hours from my surgery, I was really struggling and placed in a medical induced coma. I spent the next six days in this situation, with the first couple of days being clouded by the uncertainty of whether I would survive.

With the amazing support of Nerissa (my now wife) and family, I pulled through this terrifying event, and to much of the doctors' amazement, I was released from hospital in around 3.5 weeks. I had two major milestones I wanted to achieve:
1. Nerissa and I getting married on December 14 that same year of 2002 - achieved
2. Return to AFL football - achieved 6 June 2003.

My first interaction with the KIDS Foundation was after I returned to AFL training with North Melbourne in January 2003. My mailbox at the Football Club was full of information pamphlets about the KIDS Foundation and a lovely letter from CEO, Susie O'Neill. Susie has so much passion for the Foundation and is relentless in her endeavour to help people less fortunate that eventually we connected. I immediately committed to assisting with an advertising campaign for the KIDS Foundation and ultimately became an ambassador. I'm still proud to declare I hold an Ambassador role some 18 years later.

Jason and wife Nerissa with Brittney

Jason with Ashley and Bec

My wife, Nerissa, with an education in primary school teaching, left her teaching position to work for the KIDS Foundation for six years running injury prevention and recovery programs, and burn survivor camps. The foundation become a huge part of our lives in those early years post the traumatic experience of the Bali bombings, and upon reflection, assisted us greatly in our own healing process while gaining much satisfaction from helping others, predominantly children and teenagers who had unfortunately suffered from burn injuries. Both myself and Nerissa are extremely grateful of the support and association with the KIDS Foundation and in particular Susie.

Jason and Nerissa have bought happiness to many through camps and visiting young survivors in hospital, giving them hope at a time when they need it to get through that next phase of their recovery. In 2005, Nerissa and Jason were at the AFL Grand Final and were introduced to Peter and Matt Thiele who were given two tickets to the game. They were Sydney Swans supporters and were there to cheer on their team.

Jason and Brittney

The Return of a Champion

If he never wore the jumper, never again played the game,
We'd still remember him a champion, think of him the same.

When the nation's heart was bleeding,
one of our bravest stood tall.
And 88 Australians would be proud he heard the call.

At first it seemed impossible but we prayed he'd find a way.
The recovery never over, but a chapter closed that day.

A once in a lifetime hero, and for years we'll reminisce.
The tape was in and ready, I wasn't missing this.

The coach would keep us waiting, but the story
would write itself. And the shivers were purely spinal
when he stepped up from the shelf.

And from Bali ashes to the footy field, a victim was no more.
Tiger fans are passionate but would greet him with a roar.

Not only would he play a part, but would thrive footy heat.
Courage found its definition, in the man from Arden Street.

And in the climax of the battle, he turned the tide their way.
And in victory, retirement was the only thing left to say.

Even the boldest shed a tear as this fairy tale came true.
He thanked us for our support, but every Aussie knew.

That it was he who deserved the 'thank yous',
the applause, the admiration.

For a humble Jase McCartney, you are an inspiration.

by David O'Neill

You always make each day such a special day. You know how? By just your being you.

- FRED ROGERS

Matt

We were told to say our goodbyes to Matt.

Matty was just three when he was trapped in a burning car, back in April 1999. He has the cheekiest smile that couldn't be taken away, even on the day that was to change their lives forever. Doctors suggested to Matt's parents that they turn off his life support. They didn't. Matt's mum Lisa shares her story...

I had just driven to pick up my older children from school, parked in the driveway, and walked into the house expecting Matt had followed behind us. When I realised Matt wasn't there, I returned quickly to find Matt had locked all the car doors. Then I saw my worst nightmare, the car was on fire. I ran into the house to get the keys, and our gardener ran and helped me to get Matt out of the car. What followed next changed our lives forever ...

Matt suffered 30% full thickness burns mainly to his hands, arms, chest, and face. He was flown to the Royal Children's Hospital (RCH) where he spent 33 days in intensive care in an induced coma. After two weeks in intensive care, Matt had two cardiac arrests. Peter (Matt's dad) and I were told to say our goodbyes to Matt as the doctors thought he wouldn't make it through the night. He fought on for the next three days, but then the doctor in charge came and spoke to me and suggested that we think about taking him off life support. They said his quality of life was not going to be very good

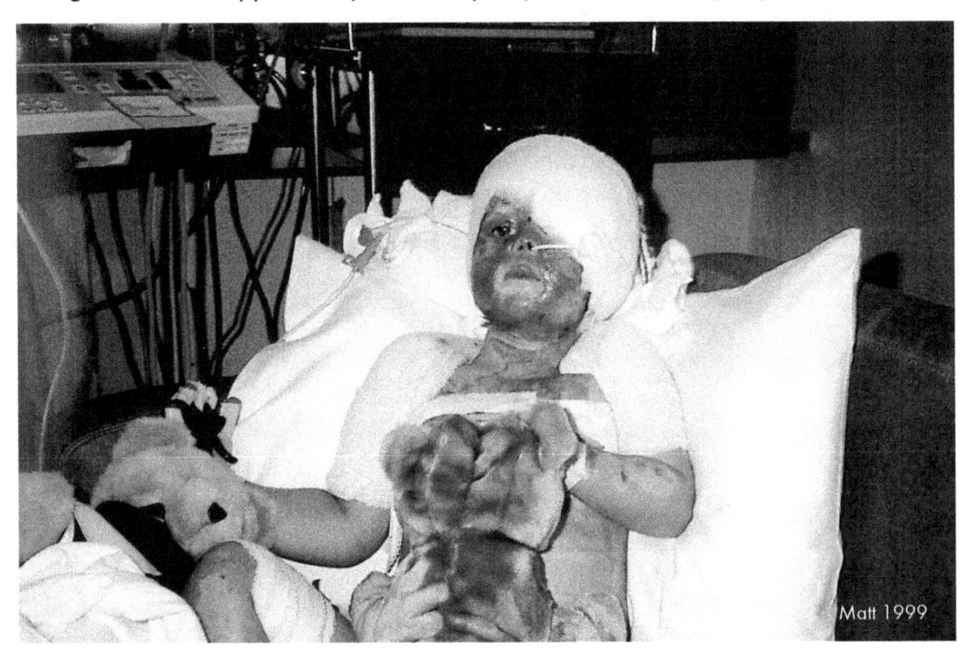

Matt 1999

as all Matt's organs had shut down and they believed that there was a degree of brain damage. The doctors asked me to make a decision even though my husband Peter was working really late that night. They said, "We can't wait for your husband. You need to tell us what you want to do." I told them that I didn't think I could do it. That was the hardest decision I have ever had to make. I told the doctor that I wanted to speak with other specialists to get their opinions so we could make an informed decision. In the end, we made the decision to not turn it off as Matt turned a corner and was able to come off some of the drugs helping to keep his heart going.

Matt was extremely shy and spent his early childhood years hidden behind me, trying to avoid the stares and attention of inquisitive strangers. Matt would walk through a shopping centre and hide behind me, people would stop, crowd around, and stare. His self-esteem was so low, down to nothing. Most of the time, people weren't really trying to hurt us, and a couple of times they thought he actually had a mask on. One time, we were walking through a shopping centre when one lady walked up to Matt and asked, "What happened to your face?" It is really painful for a parent to hear the ignorance of some; they just need to be sensitive and understand how to go about tough conversations.

In 2005, we were given two AFL Grand Final tickets to see the Sydney Swans play. Peter and Matt went along to the game, and there they met Nerissa and Jason McCartney. Nerissa was working with the KIDS Foundation at the time and suggested that we go to a Burn Survivors' family camp that was coming up in a couple of months. Peter mentioned it to me when they got home from celebrating the Sydney Swans winning the grand finale. We decided it was too short notice to go to the camp that year. Peter wasn't sure about whether it was worth going, but I was determined to make it to the next one. It was our first camp in 2006, and we were going to Tangalooma. I was pretty nervous when we got to the ferry as everyone seemed to know each other and were like a big family. It was a great camp, and I couldn't believe how much Matt seemed to blossom throughout the weekend. It was amazing to meet other survivors and how everyone saw Matt and looked beyond his scars. Matt loved the camp and seeing the difference it made to him, Peter and I then wanted to keep going to the camps. I realised now why

Daniel Macpherson and Matt

Leanne, Lisa and Matt

everyone seemed to be like family, and we are now a part of that. Susie would often ask if Matt could go to different fundraisers and functions to say a little speech or to just thank people for their fundraising. What started out as little speeches soon grew, and Matt could confidently get up and speak in front of large crowds. I'm so proud of the person Matt has become. He is a real inspiration to everyone he meets and also the younger burn survivors. They think, "Wow, if Matt can do that, why can't I!" The camaraderie between them all is awesome. Matt has now found his confidence and self-esteem thanks to the KIDS Foundation. Matt's reflection...

My parents had to make a decision to keep me alive with the possibility of me having brain damage and not being able to walk, run, or be a normal kid, or to pull the plug and let me go. Luckily, I have no memories, and the choice they made meant I'm here today.

When I was three years old, I was involved in a car fire. I suffered 30% full thickness burns and was flown to the Royal Children's Hospital. The burns were predominantly to my hands and face. I've been told only stories of what it was like for me in hospital. I had machines working for me to keep me alive and was on lots of medication. Luckily, I have no memories of my time in hospital, as I'm sure it was quite an ordeal. I am thankful that I don't remember. I got so bad at one point that the doctors did not think I would survive, and if I did, I would not have a very good quality of life. So, the doctors came to my parents with a hard decision. This was a decision they had to make quickly, and in the end, they decided to keep my life support on. Eventually, I began to recover quite remarkably in such a short amount of time, I was taken off life support systems and most of my medication. This was not the end. I had to endure surgery after surgery. They needed to add grafts to my scarred skin as this was the only way my skin was able to stretch with my body as I grew. This can be painful, but it is the only way for me to gain increased movement and a wider range of motion. This would become a lifelong thing as I would constantly need operations to relieve tight skin as I grew up.

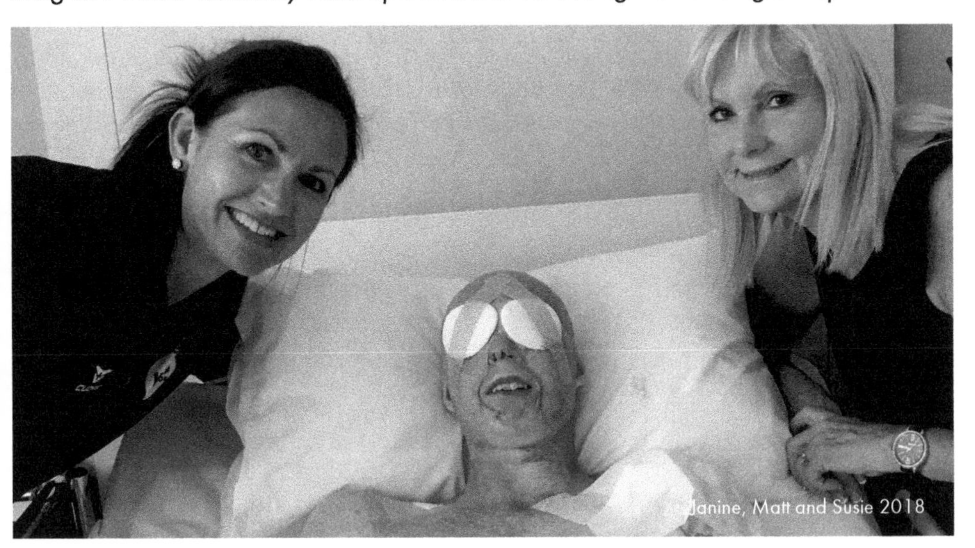

Janine, Matt and Susie 2018

I had to also relearn how to walk and talk, which required a range of specialists. My fingers were so badly burnt that the doctors had to amputate the ends of my fingers that were no longer salvageable, so I had to get used to different movements and ways of picking up and holding things. This was a long journey, and while we were allowed to be home, there were constant trips back and forth to the hospital to do more surgeries and all sorts of appointments with doctors and therapists.

Growing up, I had very little confidence and self-esteem, as I was very aware of my appearance and how others saw me. This grew to the point where I would not like to go outside as I feared the points and stares from people who did not know what had happened, not to mention some of the comments made by kids and adults. It made me feel very uncomfortable. My life up until about 10 was pretty much going to places I felt safe, like church and school, and avoiding going anywhere I didn't have to. When I went to the shopping centre, it was like I was on show. I would constantly see people staring and hear people make comments. People were inquisitive and came up to me and said things like, "What happened to your face?" or something of that nature.

My mum and dad found out about an organisation that had a yearly camp for people like me who had burns. We went along to a KIDS Foundation - Burn Survivors' Camp not really knowing what to expect, but that's when my life changed. When I saw all these other burn survivors, I realised that I wasn't the only one. It was a revelation. All these kids my age and older people that had survived their burns, doing all these activities and just having fun. From then on, I realised that going outside is something I can deal with, and that is when I thought I'm going to do this too, and when I began to live my life. From that day on, I went out and was much more comfortable with my scars, because that's who I am. I have so much I can do and give, just the way I am.

There is this indescribable brotherhood among us. You instantly get a very big sense of belonging. I got that boost I needed for my confidence and self-esteem. Ever since then, I've become a part of this big family, and they a part of mine. We have this tight bond, life-long friendships, and all stay connected, whether that's through our Zoom group chats arranged by KIDS, Facebook, or email. Then we all get to catch-up at the camps and have the best time, being challenged doing things that take us outside our

Susie and Matt Hamilton Island

comfort zone (Susie is good at that), learning life skills, or just doing whatever we like. It took me a good two or three years of going to camp to really begin to come out of my shell. I see it a lot with the younger burn survivors that come to their first camp. They pretty much go through exactly the same as I did. They start off really shy and closed off, and then the next time you see them they're much happier, more confident, and comfortable being around people and more importantly comfortable with themselves.

I have a really great group of mates, and we get to do all the things young adults do. If I'm at the movies with friends or family, I don't really care as much now about the stares. I tend to just smile, and if they want to know more, I'm happy to share my story. It is funny how people think you are incapable of doing things though. I'd rather people didn't assume that I can't do things because of the way I look. There is really nothing I can't do. I didn't get into a lot of sports in my younger years, but one thing I did do on my first camp was a karate session on the beach. Susie will explain this story too as it was my first time meeting the lovely founder of the KIDS Foundation. Now I was very shy, but I joined into all the activities. It was really fun, and I enjoyed myself. We then finished with a game where we split into pairs. After a while, I ended up with my face down, almost eating sand as a result of someone falling on top of me. This was the founder of the KIDS Foundation. That experience did not turn me off karate, as I later pursued it. It was another great tool for my confidence. It was also great for my physiotherapy and helped me improve stretch and balance. I kept up karate until I eventually got to my black belt, which is one great achievement I am proud of to this day.

A few years after my first camp, I was approached by Susie and asked if I was able to share my story at a fundraiser they were having. At this point, I was still very much a shy person either by nature or as a result of the accident, and the thought of talking in front of a crowd was pretty daunting. We went along to that event, and public speaking turned out to be very good for me in terms that it was another way of me getting out there and learning to accept this thing that had happened to me and own it. From there, the speaking engagements grew to more and bigger functions as the KIDS Foundation gained more awareness.

I've now been involved with the KIDS Foundation for 15 years, and I'm proud to be a Youth Ambassador for the Foundation, as well as a mentor to young burn survivors. It's going really well, and I love helping people find their confidence again, like I found mine here. When I go on the camps, I'm usually buddied with a young survivor. When we buddy with someone, we're with them the whole time. On some camps, the parents aren't there, so we're looking after them essentially. The most horrifying burn survivor story that I've heard was when I was buddied with a young boy, Fletcher. He and his brother Spencer were deliberately burnt by their father who is now in jail. Their mum has remarried, and their stepfather is a good father figure for them.

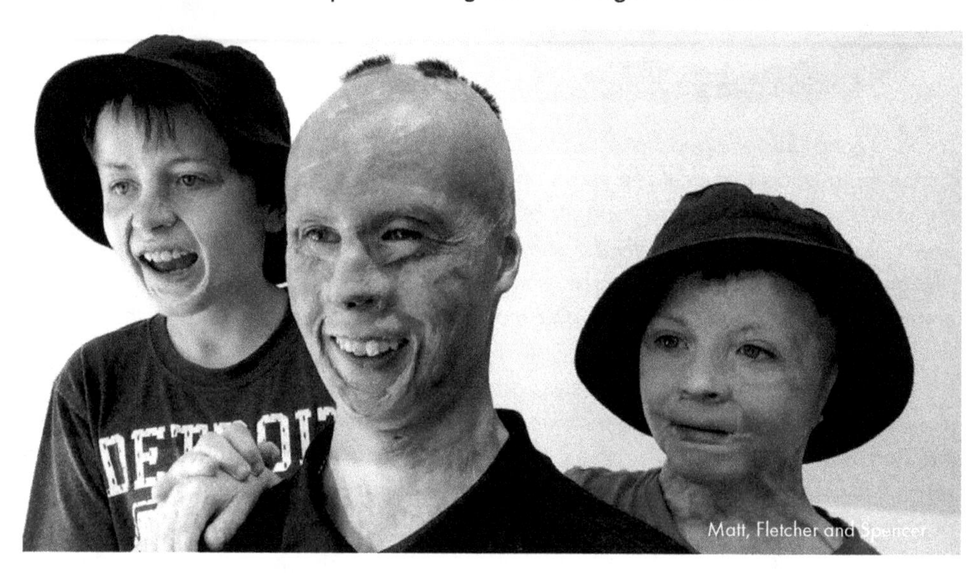

Matt, Fletcher and Spencer

It's safe to say that the Foundation has been a real life changer, and I really would not be where and who I am without them. I now have my own vending machine business and my own house, and I'm free to go out and hang with friends and catch up with the family instead of shutting everything out and not doing anything. My future is a much brighter place now, and I can't wait to see what it brings.

Matt has been on a tough and emotional journey but is not one to feel sorry for himself. He is one of the happiest young men around, always quick with a smile and enjoys life. As Matt mentioned, we first meet under the most unusual circumstances during a karate lesson. We were playing a game of tag, and I fell backwards, landing on top of Matt and face planting him into the sand. I felt so bad, but Matt just spat out the sand and brushed his face then gave me the biggest smile. "I'm okay," he said. I replied with, "I hope you never go on to get your black belt. I might just be in trouble," and he did. One of our favourite activities at camp is the karate sessions Matt takes in the mornings usually on a beach somewhere.

Matt's karate session at Camp Phoenix

I have watched him gain many new friends, dramatically improve his confidence and self-esteem, and grow into the most delightful young man. At his 21st birthday, I was very emotional. You would have thought he was one of my own children. Well in a way, he is a big part of my extended family.

Matt finds it difficult to attempt new challenges. He has a fairly defined comfort zone and massive fear of the unknown, no wonder with what he has gone through. That does not stop us to push him a little, and he does give it a big red hot go, most times! The first time was getting Matt to join us on a tube behind a boat at a Hamilton Island camp. His dad was very excited when he heard the news, as they owned a boat and Matt had never ventured past the observer seat. On one particular occasion, we were sand tobogganing and tramped up the big hill on Moreton Island, preparing to come down the other side, but when he reached the top and saw what was ahead of him, he quickly changed his mind. So, we pushed him a little, literally. Twenty-five minutes later with blood dripping from his knuckles through the deadly grip, hanging on so tight, he gave in and allowed the instructor to let go and give him that gentle push. We all fell to the ground from sheer exhaustion, but it was well worth it to see that smile when we all reached the bottom. On another occasion, we were at the water park in Queenscliff and there was a waterslide. Twenty-five minutes later he allowed us to let the tube go, and this picture tells it all.

Susie, Belinda and Matt at the Noosa Tri

For years, Matt had been volunteering as part of the KIDS Noosa Tri Crew, attending functions and cheering on the KIDS team. KIDS Foundation is one of the Noosa Triathlon Charity Partners and has a group of triathletes that race for KIDS and fundraise to promote our cause. One of our very loyal competitors and fundraisers, Janet Miller, always boasting a smile nearly as big as Matt's, inspired and challenged Matt to join her in a team the following year. This was way outside his comfort zone, but Matt surprisingly accepted. Janet was to do the 1.5km swim leg, I was taking on the 40km bike leg, and Matt the 10km run. He had never run before, but he trained for a year to be able to take on this new challenge. We had a great day, and to see Matt finish, still boasting that beautiful smile, even in the toughest stages of the course, was overwhelming and brought a tear to eye of the many people watching.

Our latest challenge is to appear on Adventure All Stars in 2021. In August, Matt, Michelle Harris (another KIDS supporter), and myself have formed a team to personally raise $30,000 and take on a week of challenges to be filmed through the Charity TV Global. I'm so proud of what Matt has achieved, his business, home, the beautiful friendships he has and has made, and these challenges that keep on keeping on.

Matt at Dolphin Marine Conservation Park Coffs Harbour

Successful mothers are
not the ones that
have never struggled.
They are the ones
that never give up,
despite the struggles.

- SHARON JAYNES

Mums

Sharing our unique stories gives inspiration to others to help reduce their pain.

While in many cases the children can be so resilient and move forward in a positive way, their parents or the person that was caring for them at the time of the incident cannot. It is common to sit in a group session with the mums at a camp and listen to them pour out feelings of guilt and talk about the post-traumatic stress that has consumed their lives. It is equally as important to have great support programs in place for the parents and carers, as it is for their children. There are times when the really rewarding activity that bonds the parent, grandparent, or carer with the child ends in an unexpected tragedy, something that never leaves them. Often with burns, the visual change to their loved one's appearance is a constant reminder.

Camp Phoenix Tangalooma

The reason why you need
emotional support is because it's
important for survivors to be heard.
To be understood.
To be able to express yourself without
fearing criticism or harsh judgement.
To be validated for your pain,
suffering, and loss.
For others to be there for you to
encourage you, especially if you're
having a bad day or feeling triggered.

- DANA ARCURI

Families

Supporting survivors of burns, accidents, attacks, crime, neglect, abuse, and environmental events.

Everyday members of the team at the KIDS Foundation devote their time and resources to help survivors and their families rebuild their lives. While nurturing each little person's needs during their recovery, we are also consciously supporting the healthy development of family relationships. Traumatic events can cause stress responses in other family members, which impede on their relationships and ideal family functioning. It is equally important to support the family as one, as well as addressing individual needs, because it aids the recovery of everyone within the family that is struggling in different ways.

On the last day of one of our fundraising trips where we rode from Coffs Harbour to Noosa, we came across a family playing at a playground in Eumundi. The mum came up to us and asked who we were and about the KIDS Foundation. After a long chat, she asked if we had ever thought about including children with other injuries from traumatic circumstances other than burns. Her son had been attacked by a dog causing facial scaring and emotional trauma. KIDS Foundation had a recovery arm, and opportunity to expand the support to other children who experienced harm and injuries outside burns seemed timely. This sector of the Foundation has continued to grow and has encouraged hospitals and medical professionals to introduce us to some wonderful families.

Although many of our survivors have injuries related to scalds or burns which are often quite visual, many have internal scars. Our recovery programs are not only designed to support survivors of burns, but other serious accidents, caused by dog attacks, crime, neglect, abuse, and environmental events.

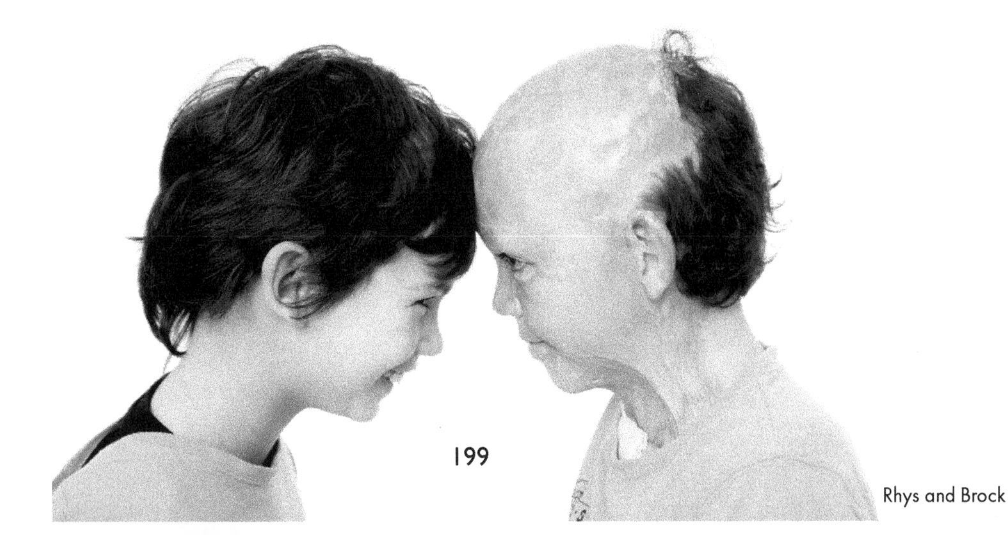

Rhys and Brock

Real pleasure comes
from overcoming challenges,
feeling confidence
in your abilities,
and experiencing the
power this brings.

- ROBERT GREENE

The beeping of the machines breathing for her and the twice weekly surgeries were harrowing. I have few photos of the early days in ICU; however, the images are etched in my mind forever. Natasha's story through the words of mum, Zoi...

My beautiful daughter Natasha was four months shy of her fourth birthday when she was taken to The Royal Children's Hospital on May 26, 2011. She was involved in a terrible accident in the kitchen at my mother's home. Natasha was cooking with her grandmother, as she had done many times before. She was perched up, sitting on the kitchen bench beside the stovetop, when she leaned too close to the open flame and her dress caught on fire. The frantic calls of my mother to get help and the voicemails she left me will stay in my psyche forever. At the time when the ambulance arrived, Natasha's injures seemed less intense than they subsequently became, as unbeknown to me, burns continue to burn for days after the initial injury.

After our initial first traumatic days in ICU, we were told that Natasha had sustained full thickness burns to roughly 50% of her body, including her face and head. We spent five weeks in ICU. Four of those Natasha was intubated, wrapped like a mummy, swollen, and unrecognisable. Her feet where the only thing that I recognised and the only part of her I could hold. Looking back now, I shudder still at the thought of those 16 weeks in hospital. The beeping of the machines breathing for her and the twice weekly surgeries were harrowing. I have few photos of the early days in ICU; however, the images are etched in my mind forever.

Natasha has a sister Chloe who is 13 months younger, and she was also on my mind. Knowing the guilt of leaving her with other family members was also a deep pain. The road to recovery was long, painful, and extremely challenging. Learning to walk again after weeks of being immobile in bed, learning how to eat again after months of a gastric tube feeding, Morphine, fentanyl, so much for a tiny body to manage. Any chance I had I would be in the hospital library researching food for healing, best foods for skin, etc. Natasha was a slight build already but had lost weight and was disinterested in food, often vomiting what she was being feed. There were many tears and some tantrums but mostly fear in my baby's eyes that were heartbreaking to see. I wished with everything in my bones that I could protect her from any further pain, knowing I couldn't break me. I had to stay strong, stoic, and fearless for her, but inside I was falling apart.

On week 14, we were sent home armed with bandages, pain, sleep and nerve medication, and pressure garments that Natasha needed to now wear 24/7. She was brave and compliant with these, although I struggled with her mask, we all became accustomed. We slowly made our way back into some degree of normality. Natasha went back to kinder for a couple of days as she got stronger. There were challenges with her skin not healing, and I became well versed in changing bandages. Sometimes I would look at her and not recognise my little girl. Everything seemed different about her and of course it was. What she had endured would of course change anyone, let alone a small child.

The next challenge was dealing with the public attention. I became expert at not focusing on people around us and their stares. It never ceased to amaze me the degree of insensitivity by adults who would unconsciously make faces as they walked by and stared. The children I could deal with as they were innocently curious and just needed a small explanation. Natasha was oblivious for a while until she got a little older. I could suddenly see her awareness click in. This was difficult to watch as she started to become awakened to the fact that she was different. I enrolled her in dancing the following year after her accident, as I thought she could start to make some local friends and the activity would be a kind of physio for her. She absolutely loved it, and it has been a constant source of joy ever since. She is now 160cm tall and hasn't required skin releases, which we think is partly because of all the dancing she has done these last nine years.

I had known about the KIDS Foundation while I was in the hospital researching for anything burns related that would be helpful. I shelved it to the back of my mind as I felt completely overwhelmed by the idea of meeting other families, I was struggling to deal with my own reality. It wasn't until Natasha turned seven that we made contact and connected with the KIDS Foundation. It was time for us to come together with other families who have experienced similar heartache, so we registered for our first Camp

Ana, Natasha, Matt, Chloe, Varli, Fletcher, Spencer

Phoenix. It was a challenging but inspiring time connecting with beautiful, generous of heart people and meeting the divine Susie O'Neill and being welcomed to what has become our second family. The KIDS Foundation and the camps have been amazing experiences, for not only Natasha, but also her younger sister and me. It has given both children a sense of home, where they know that they will be loved, understood, and supported. We have since attended many camps as a family, and Natasha has been a participant at the kids only camps. She has made great friends.

Natasha started high school last year. It's a scary and exciting time as she is growing into a young woman and I can see her self-doubt and insecurities. Whatever the challenges, we will walk through them together as she has chosen me to be her mum in this lifetime, and I am privileged she has.

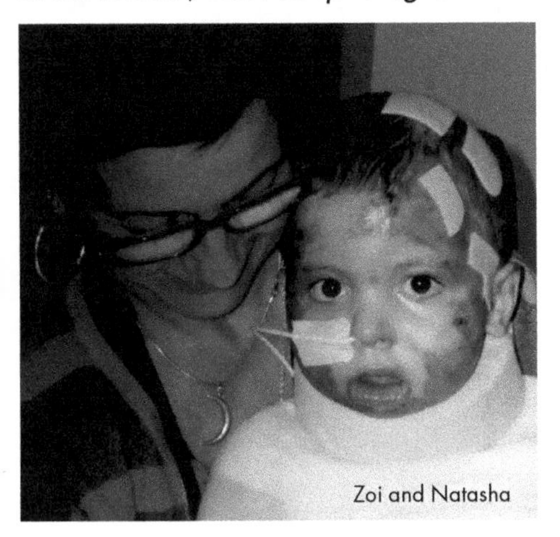
Zoi and Natasha

Chloe and Natasha

I remember when this photo was taken, Natasha and I were in the playroom, and I was finally allowed to hold her and have her sit on my lap for a little while. I look at the photo now and remember the hours she endured, the many procedures and skin grafting operations, and having to learn to walk and eat again after being immobile for so long and being feed via a tube. Looking at her now, I can see how the strength of her spirit and the KIDS Foundation got all of us through that time. Thank you from all our hearts.

Healing doesn't mean the damage never existed. It means the damage no longer controls our lives.

- UNKNOWN

The nightmares just wouldn't go away.

There is one little girl that I love dearly that entered the Foundation in 2016. For the purpose of this story, we will call her Gabby. She had gone to play with a friend when she passed by the home of a person with special needs. This man enticed her into his home, attempted to rape her, and repeatedly stabbed her 30 times narrowly missing her heart. She was five years old at the time. Fortunately, Gabby escaped, ran for help, and was taken by ambulance to hospital in a serious condition where she underwent surgery to save her life.

For years, Gabby had horrific nightmares. She would sit in the lounge room too scared to sleep, and then eventually around 2 a.m. out of sheer tiredness would fall asleep on the couch. This was not an ideal situation for a little girl who had to be at school by 9 a.m. that morning. So, one day we went around to her house and involved Gabby in making her bedroom a safe place. The room looked beautiful featuring a salt lamp, soft music, and toys to give her comfort. KIDS Foundation's mascot SeeMore Safety sat proudly on her bed. SeeMore's name printed on the t-shirt glows in the dark, and she was eager to see this when the lights were out.

Her mum rang me the next morning, so excited to share the news that for the first time since her incident she had slept in her own room and does so to this day. I visited her just before Christmas to deliver some gifts. The COVID-19 pandemic has prevented us from running our camps, but that has not stopped us for caring for these children and doing whatever we can to make sure their lives are the best they can be.

Injuries that leave a scar
on the outside are
often easier to understand,
than the injuries that
are invisible,
but they still hold pain.

- DR. SUSIE O'NEILL

Maggie

It may sound like a cliche', but on Friday the 13th of July 2018, our family's lives changed forever. Jayne, Maggie's mum shares their story...

Travelling home after a family holiday to Phillip Island to see the penguins, our vehicle was hit from behind as we sat stationary in congested traffic on the Western Freeway. Moments prior to this occurring, our seven-year-old daughter Maggie was curious to know if we would arrive home in time for her to watch her favourite TV show Better Homes and Gardens. Maggie had just dozed off to sleep after a few big fun-filled days on the beach, enjoying the last of the July school holidays.

It was without warning and not until we ended up on the grassy embankment of the Western Freeway, clipping the rear of the vehicle in front of us, that we realised that we had been hit from behind and catapulted forward by a vehicle travelling at 100 kms behind us. Our teenage boy was conscious and responsive, but Maggie was unresponsive, bent over, and slumped in her seat with no apparent signs of life. We dragged her from the car onto the side of the road where we kept her breathing, blood draining from her ears and mouth, until the paramedics arrived. There began our greatest journey ever - every second passing feeling like an eternity of pain, petrified that Maggie would die on the side of the road that night. Maggie was stabilised while on the roadside before being transferred into the road ambulance, incubated, and transported to the HEMS helicopter for transit to the Royal Children's Hospital. The trip for her was barely six minutes, but for us, separated from her and wondering whether she had survived, it felt like an eternity as we were escorted by police car. We were faced with the unknown when we reached the hospital. We were told to brace ourselves for the worst by the members of the trauma team, as we were unable to be with Maggie until she was more stable. We had never set foot into RCH, and ironically, only three days earlier, as we drove via the city to our holiday destination, we had expressed our gratitude that we hadn't needed to.

Chris and Maggie

From that day, we began a long and intense relationship with the hospital and staff, which will continue until Maggie's adulthood, where she will then commence a new relationship with an appropriate adult facility. For the seven days following the accident, we sat by Maggie's bedside in ICU, completely powerless to do anything for Maggie medically (that was the incredible responsibility of the remarkable staff in the emergency and ICU departments), but frantically we attempted to come to terms with the situation. One full of the unknown, worst case scenario fears, and what her and our lives would look like into the future. The other reality that we were facing was that it could have happened to any family on that day, but for no reason at all, except being in the "wrong place at the wrong time," it happened to us. The safety and predictability of the life that we had known and planned had been torn away, and it was terrifying in every way.

The abundance of support and love offered to us was beyond our comprehension. Never had we required prayers, love, and support like we did during this time, and fortunately, we received, in absolute abundance. Again, the staff at the Royal Children's Hospital were our lifeline to the little girl we had known and the now altered version of the girl we would learn to know and continue to do so today. Maggie underwent numerous surgeries over the next few months, including a reconstruction of the right-hand side of her precious face, several surgeries to her right eye to ensure she didn't lose it, and then to attempt to ensure it would open and fully function. Maggie had many other procedures during her initial recovery including a blood transfusion, brain monitoring equipment inserted, CT scans, MRIs, and many other procedures. These were all to aid in keeping her alive and then to assist her in recovery, too many procedures to recall, it seems trauma does that to your memory, eliminates the ability to keep count of the constant medical interventions that have been required.

Our Maggie has now been left with an Acquired Brain Injury (ABI), permanent damage to her right frontal lobe that will not allow her brain to ever function as it did prior to the impact of the accident. She continuously struggles with many daily challenges that come as a direct result from the accident - an inability to regulate her emotions at times and often becoming fixated on different subjects throughout the day. Her anxieties and concerns about people, objects, or tasks are often irrational and can't be soothed. Sometimes this extends to paranoia, and more often than not, severe anxiety and the inability to control her behaviour and emotions. Maggie now has great difficulty with relationship building, maintaining, navigating, and understanding them. Maggie requires constant reassurance and as much predictability in her day-to-day life as possible so that she can gain a sense of control. Unfortunately, life now presents as a "rollercoaster" for both Maggie and the people who know and love her.

We as a family bare the deep emotional scars of the incident and the reality of the past, current, and the unknown future. We continue to be strongly supported by professionals and "our people," but the ongoing court proceedings, driven by the justice system and the capacity of the accused to require us to keep retelling and reliving our story of heart break and pain, layers our trauma more heavily. We will always rely on others for support (emotional and practical), understanding, and education we know we can't do it alone. It's a community that assists us just like the community that we met through the KIDS Foundation in 2019. We were invited to a KIDS Family Camp in Noosa as a result of a previously established relationship that I had with Susie O'Neill (Founder and CEO of KIDS Foundation) via her daughter. I was aware of the Foundation and the wonderful work they carried out. I had in the past competed in fun runs to help raise money for the charity, but always thought KIDS was only for burn survivors.

Our first camp was challenging. Maggie doesn't have any visible scars or physical disability from her accident or the trauma. Her wounds are deep though, as are ours after experiencing such a significant trauma. The camp was a safe place (often there is an absence of safe places for Maggie), but at the KIDS camp, she could be present and behave without judgement. I, too, could be well supported and importantly heard, and Maggie could be understood and honoured for being her. We continue our relationship with the KIDS Foundation, and I am extremely grateful for the nurturing and support it provides for Maggie and our family. Our stories may all be different, but many of our trauma experiences are shared, and at the very least, understood and valued!

Maggie

To be a star, you must shine
your own light,
follow your own path,
and don't worry about darkness,
for that is when the
stars shine brightest.

- NAPOLEON HILL

Tianna

The chance of survival was very small. 26 years later, I'm writing my story to inspire others.

Children come and go depending on where they are at in life. Tianna first came to the KIDS Foundation in 2003 when she was just 10 years old. In 2019, Tianna returned as a participant and volunteer. Her role had been put on pause in 2020 due to COVID-19, but 2021 brings new opportunities to Tianna, some quite beyond her comfort zone.

My name is Tianna-Joy, I am a burn survivor. In 1994, my bedroom night light caught my wall on fire in the middle of the night. I was 14 months old at the time. My mum woke up to me crying, opened my door, and saw me crawling on the floor in flames. I was airlifted to hospital with serious injuries. The smoke had blown holes in my lungs and my windpipe was destroyed. The flames had taken my toes and heels, and I had third and fourth degree burns to 69% of my body. The doctors told my mum I wouldn't be able to survive this. The chance of survival was very small. 26 years later I'm writing my story to inspire anyone who's reading Susie's book. I met Susie a very long time ago. It was 2003, and it was my very first burn camp where as a little girl, I finally felt like I belonged somewhere. Growing up was hard, but as a burn survivor, growing up was even harder. Feeling like I was the only one with burns was a struggle, but then my mum, who has been my rock and lifesaver throughout my journey since day one, needed support herself. She was struggling, the whole family was struggling, so she found the wonderful, one and only KIDS Foundation. We attended this family camp/retreat with my brother and sister joining, and we were all supported. I don't remember much about my first camp, but what I do remember is feeding dolphins with my mum (Antoinette), Susie, and Shannon. Shannon was a Big Brother contestant and my buddy at camp. For some reason, I had in my head these were not dolphins. I thought they were sharks.

Tianna, Shannon and Susie feeding dolphins at Camp Phoenix Tangalooma

I was so scared, I spent most of the time crying, having a crazy idea that I was being fed to the sharks. I look back now and laugh, especially considering the dolphins were very therapeutic and often considered an important part of our recovery program at camp. We felt part of a big family, and despite the dolphin episode, being in a safe place and not being judged meant the world to us. Our family was part of a special burn survivor community that helped us in many ways. But I still suffered really badly from social anxiety. I felt like the whole world was staring at my scars, judging my every move, so I chose to keep to myself. Up until 2017, I had isolated myself in my house. I didn't leave the house unless I was with my mum or best friend. My mum took me to the World Burns Congress (WBC) Conference in America ran by the Phoenix Society. It runs an annual conference where burn survivors, their loved ones, professional carers, researchers, and others committed to empowering the burn community come together. Although I still struggle from the fear of judgement and anxiety that really creeps in at times, it has helped me cope with those issues on occasions.

The WBC Conference in America is an initiative of the Phoenix Society. Founded by Alan Breslau in 1977, the Phoenix Society is a not-for-profit organisation dedicated to empowering people from all around the world affected by a burn injury. The Foundation was established after Alan, a burn survivor of a 1963 airplane crash, went to visit a young boy in a burn centre. There he saw the transformative power of peer support and created the Phoenix Society. I had the pleasure of meeting Delwyn, Alan's wife, at a 2018 burns support group in Queensland. Delwyn met Alan after her son was injured in an explosion in 1984, sustaining burns to 40% of his body. Her personal experience led her passion and established the Burn Support Group Charitable Trust in Auckland in 1987. Delwyn went on to marry Alan in 1993 and emigrated to the United States. She took on the role as Associate Director of the Phoenix Society, establishing the first summer camp for children who had survived a burn injury, Camp Susquehanna. Delwyn has given over 350 public presentations as well as numerous television, radio, and media interviews in the United States of America, Australia, China, and New Zealand.

Giselle, Brodie, Shannon, Nick, Tianna and David

Alan and Delwyn retired from their directorships of the Phoenix Society in 1997. An award was established in their honour, "The Alan and Delwyn Breslau Award." Sadly, Alan passed away on November 26, 2020. He will always be remembered for his long-term commitment, strong dedication, and desire to help others in the global burns survivor's community.

Although Tianna hadn't been engaged with the Foundation for some time, she felt it was time to reconnect. She felt there was more we could support her with, but equally important, she had something to give from her experiences.

Tianna

Eighteen years later, I decided to reconnect and came back to the KIDS Foundation. I wanted to become a volunteer and find ways to support this special charity. I then went on to become a KIDS leader/mentor, and I've never looked back. I remember in 2019 when I started volunteering at the very first Adelaide camp, I don't think I spoke for the first few hours I was so nervous, but then I opened up and fitted right in. The KIDS Foundation has given me so much. I have been given so much confidence and acceptance to last a lifetime and a family that will 100% be a part of me until the end. I really wouldn't be the woman I am today if I was never introduced to KIDS and that's a fact!!

I have since been lucky enough to be invited to be part of a TV show called Adventure All Stars where other KIDS Foundation members and I will take on an adventure of a lifetime and at the same time raise $10,000 for the charity. I thought this was way beyond my capability, but I have raised most of it, just in the first few months. Being on television is way out of my comfort zone, a huge step for me, but I'm going to give it my best, and that's what matters the most.

Life will have terrible blows,
horrible blows, unfair blows,
doesn't matter.
And some people recover
and others don't.

- CHARLIE MUNGER

Rebecca

"I Believe I Can Fly"

Like for many, the Coronavirus pandemic has proved to be quite a challenging time for the young people supported by the Foundation. We had a few pretty tough emotional weeks, especially those living in the lock-down areas of Melbourne. It was with great sadness that we said goodbye to 29-year-old Bec at her virtual funeral. Despite the intense physical pain of a burn injury, there is sometimes also the loss of a family member, as well as undergoing a dramatic change in body or facial image, which brings unbearable psychological trauma.

Tragic circumstances led Bec and her family to our Foundation about 15 years ago. The four children were travelling home through the Melbourne suburb of Cranbourne after a weekend visit with their father when the car in which they were travelling burst into flames. A lit cigarette ignited leaking gas from a faulty LPG gas system. They managed to escape the flames, with severe burns and witnessing the most horrific scene that ultimately claimed the life of one of the children a month later. Bec's health and emotional journey is one that she battled since that day. Bec had a beautiful self-trained voice. Her dream was to one day record a song. Her dream came true in 2010 when she recorded "I Believe I Can Fly" with Liz Gaunt (her KIDS buddy) on a KIDS album, which was a dedication to Bec and her remarkable story. The album featured Guy Sebastian, Bachelor Girl, Pete Murray, Frankie J Holden, and many more.

Elizabeth and Rebecca

*In life you get what you put in.
When you make a positive
impact in someone else's life,
you also make a positive
impact in your own life.*

- MARC AND ANGEL

CHAPTER SEVEN

Special People

Special People, Special Partners.

Appearing on current affair programs and other lifestyle shows has really helped to raise the KIDS profile connect us with wonderful ambassadors, one being Chris Scott. One day out of the blue, I received a call from a guy named Chris. The call went something like ... "Hi is that Susie O'Neill from the KIDS Foundation? My name is Chris Scott. I was watching TV with my partner Sarah and came across a story on the '7.30 Report' that featured your Foundation, and we were wondering how we could get involved." As it turned out, Chris was an AFL player, best known then for being a dual premiership player with the Brisbane Lions. Chris invited me to meet him and Sarah at the Gabba. They were really lovely, and Chris thought that with his AFL profile they might be able to help us raise money for the Foundation. That year we were given a Brisbane Lions home game at the Gabba to shake tins and raise money. The children attending a camp on the Sunshine Coast were over-the-moon with excitement when they were invited to form a guard of honour at the game and even more so when they got to go to the rooms afterwards and meet the players. It was back in 2007 when we formed a partnership with Brisbane Lions. This was about the same time Chris and Luke Power began their long-time ambassadorship with KIDS. Chris's association with the Foundation grew stronger when he was appointed as senior coach for the Geelong Cats on October 15, 2010. The KIDS head office is in Ballarat, about an hour from Geelong. This meant that we were able to engage Chris at suitable times that didn't require him travelling too far, as most events were in Melbourne or Geelong. Each year up until the COVID-19 restrictions, Chris has been the host and keynote speaker of an annual function that raises much needed funds for the KIDS Foundation.

Chris Scott and Ryan

My involvement with the KIDS Foundation, and Susie O'Neill, started toward the end of my playing career with the Brisbane Lions. I'd had a successful career by most measures and had been very fortunate to be a part of a great organisation and successful on-field team. In the latter half of my 14 years with the Brisbane Lions, I was plagued by injury. Often, I was able to play, sometimes not, but rarely was I pain free. It was a constant struggle to come up for training and games, and it was difficult to avoid the downward spiral of self-pity.

It was in this context that my soon to be wife Sarah and I were watching the 7.30 Report on the ABC one night. A remarkable lady was talking about the work she was doing with young people who had suffered serious injury, primarily burns. It was over 15 years ago, but I am still moved by the emotions this story generated in us. Anyone who has had even the slightest burn can attest to the pain. To then consider suffering burns to the majority of your body, requiring surgery after surgery to graft skin all the while being in unimaginable pain. As horrific as this thought is, and as this story has explained so emotionally, it isn't the worst part of these types of injuries. The psychological trauma associated with looking different to other kids and dealing with the insensitivity of people who are surprised by your appearance is immense.

This quickly gave me a sense of perspective. Susie and KIDS Foundation gave me much more than I could give them. At the least, I thought I'd see what I could do. I hunted down Susie's contact details and began a relationship with KIDS that, while I hope it's helped them a bit, has made me a much more compassionate and empathetic person.

You're an inspiration Susie.

Most of our corporate partnerships have continued beyond 10 years. One actually ran over a 23-year period, and our branding continues on their products today. It is usually the passion of one individual within a company that champions the partnership. This is like gold to a charity but also a weakness, as it is the reason our partnerships have ceased, because when that person moves on from the company, the new person in that role brings along their own associated charities.

Camp Phoenix

Success is not measured in
the amount of dollars you make,
but the amount of lives you impact.

- UNKNOWN

COTTON ON FOUNDATION

As a corporate partner, we felt we received so much more than what we gave.

When KIDS was first established back in 1993, we were known as KIDS Education and predominately funded by corporate sponsorship. There were fewer not for profits then, the corporate dollar was much easier to attract, and quite often the companies came to us. On one occasion at a camp held at Anglesea, Sam McGuane, a volunteer, invited his mate who worked for Cotton On to join us for breakfast. It was a long breakfast, as Tim Diamond manager of the Cotton On Foundation didn't leave until much later that afternoon and here he tells the story...

I first met Susie through mutual friends back in 2010 and could instantly feel the passion she had for KIDS Foundation and the cause. That passion was quickly turned into action. Early on, I wasn't sure exactly what the connection might be, so we went with whatever we possibly could to raise much needed funds for the organisation, and particularly the burn survivors' camps.

Things kicked off in May 2010, with the KIDS Foundation Ball, where we contributed Cotton On Body dressing gowns for their fundraiser, and every attendee received one for a premium price with a surprise voucher in the pocket. It was super successful, and that led to a number of other fundraising initiatives. From the Flintstones music CD in our Cotton On KIDS stores, to manufacturing the KIDS Foundation mascot "SeeMore" as a plush doll that was sold across their network. We also got involved in a number of events, particularly one epic event, the 1200km bike ride Port to Port, Port Melbourne to Port Macquarie. We tried a lot of different things and had a whole lot of fun doing it. We really felt that we had a great, close knit relationship, and that was really validated when we jointly won a Rotary Australia award for our community partnership. But for me, more important was the momentum we were gathering as valued partners.

As the Injury Prevention programs were being extended into a wider range of schools, the Burn Survivors' Network became a real passion of our partnership. Being connected to injury survivors and their families was something that's very hard to put into words. Camp TANGO in 2012 was really our first "all in" camp. We stumped up funding, had volunteers from Cotton On Head Office, and each year we supported those camps to continue on. These volunteers were so taken away with the experience, the overwhelming feedback was that they had no idea how connected and grateful they would feel for the experience. And many continued their involvement, creating a separate "KF Volunteer Group."

Cotton On staff enjoying Camp Phoenix at Angelsea

I too had the opportunity to experience a camp in Anglesea. Meeting these incredible kids and their families and seeing them engage with others in the same situation was simply incredible. It's an experience that absolutely stays with you. Overarching, the many volunteers came away with the same feeling and memories, where we, as a corporate partner, felt we received so much more than what we gave. That was a sign of a genuine, mutually beneficial partnership.

There've been so many other memories along the journey. I've always admired what Susie and KIDS Foundation stood for and how their passion never wavered. Susie knows how truly beneficial their work is and uses that passion to do more and continue to make a difference. To this day, our staff engage in volunteering and mentoring and have become great ambassadors for the KIDS Foundation. Cotton On support continues today, a partnership that has evolved and grown for more than a decade.

KIDS
FOUNDATION
Burn Survivors
NETWORK

Never underestimate the valuable
and important difference
you make in every life you touch.
For the impact you make today
has a powerful rippling
effect on every tomorrow.

- UNKNOWN

Passionate Partnership

HARRIS TRADE PLUMBING SUPPLIES

It was an experience I had as a four-year-old. The image was indelibly stamped into my brain from that young age, and I believe has always been why I have shown an interest in supporting KIDS, though I have never shared this thought before out of respect.

It was back in 1962, I was four years old, and the highlight of my days was the Harrington's bread man making his daily deliveries. My mum would often allow me to go out to the van and choose a treat, a cream bun or the like. On this particular day, I observed a boy sitting in the passenger seat who to me looked incredibly disfigured, his face looked like it had melted. I went suddenly quite when I saw him and then shied away not understanding what had happened to him or how to deal with what I saw. Afterwards, I asked my mother what had happened to this boy, and she explained he had fallen into a hot bath and had had many skin grafts since. Interestingly, I end up working in the plumbing supply industry and can remember in the 90s the plumbing industry mandating that tempering valves must be used on all new hot water applications in new homes or when replacing an old hot water service. I remember thinking at this time that if this boy had fallen into a hot bath nowadays, his life would be very different. I don't think enough is written about the dangers of untempered hot water these days. We just take it for granted that they are always installed. The big question is, are they? I am sure we have all gone to wash our hands and noticed that the hot water is way too hot. So, I ask, was a tempering valve installed?

The team from Harris with the ever so bold and kind-hearted Shane Viney, take on challenges for KIDS, participating in triathlons and bike rides raising money for the Foundation. There is the odd $10,000 that keeps popping into our account randomly during tough times like in COVID, along with Anthony's $10,000 birthday donation each year. It takes a pretty special person to turn it around and give on their birthday.

Shane Viney

Could anything be better than this -
Waking up every day knowing
that lots of people are
smiling because you
chose to impact lives,
making the world a better place.

- ANYAELE SAM CHIYSON

CONSOLIDATED PROPERTY SERVICES

The Grants - John, Mary, Eliza, Justin, and Paul, and Consolidated Property Services Team. The importance of sharing, recognising, and helping our people to grow is firmly entrenched in the Consolidated culture.

At the 2010 Port Macquarie Ironman in the crowd at the Carbo dinner, unbeknown to us was athlete Gareth Flynn. A few months later, we received an email from Gareth that asked for information on the KIDS Foundation. He was recommending us for the selected charity to the Irvine Club for their up-and-coming fundraising lunch. He sent an email that read:

"I also hope my committee share my sentiments and see yours as a worthy cause. By way of feedback, the involvement of the KIDS Foundation at the Port Macquarie Ironman was excellent. The tent and activities kept my kids interested, and the speech and performance at the Carbo Dinner, inspirational. Well done to all involved."

The Irvine Club was named in honour of Mr. Jock Irvine who held the position of 12th man for the Australian cricket team tour of India and South Africa in 1969/70. Jock is recognised at the Irvine Club as the 12th man who never played a test match. The not-for-profit club was founded in 2004 as a mates relationship building club, bringing together friends in a social environment, with an underlying purpose to make a real difference by generating funds for local charities. The inaugural function held at the Kelvin Club started with 70 guests and grew to now exceed over 400 guests and attracted some of the biggest speakers in the world.

We were successful in being selected for the lunch. It was on this occasion, that for the first time, my passionate speech had been overshadowed by Matt Thiele, all of 13 at the time, and he was invited to be the guest speaker. Now when you read the line-up of speakers that had previously spoken, Sam Newman, Rex Hunt, David "Bumble" Lloyd, Sir Ian Botham, Sir Vivian Richards, Sir Richard Hadlee, Peter FitzSimons, Dermott Brereton, Billy Brownless, Greg Ritchie, Robbie Slater, Allan Border, Kevin Sheedy, Sam Kekovich, Steve Bradbury, Tim Watson, and Stan Alves, just to name a few, this was a huge honour. Gareth had heard Matt speak at the Australian Ironman Championships Carbo night and must have really made a great impression.

Seated among the crowd was Justin and Paul Grant, who are Directors of Consolidated Property Services (Consolidated). A couple of years down the track, I received a call from one of the Directors, Eliza Hoppe, making some enquiries about the KIDS

Foundation as Consolidated were looking for a new charity to support. That was in 2012, and today they are still one of the KIDS Foundation's "Trusted, Loyal, and Kindest" partners.

In 2012, we were overwhelmed to be presented with an unexpected cheque for $10,000. We decided to put the money toward running a family camp for burn and injury survivors. The following year, the donation doubled, and we wanted to share with them an experience that demonstrated how much their kindness meant. So, we invited the Consolidated team to come along to see what we were doing with their donation.

That was the year that the Founders of Consolidated, Mary and John Grant, were part of the group that turned Tangalooma Moreton Island, Queensland into a sea of yellow. It was in August when the KIDS Foundation staff, Consolidated staff, volunteers, and the injury recovery children and their families descended on the island for Camp Phoenix 2013.

Camp Phoenix is a vital part of the recovery process for our young people and their families. The awesome volunteers/mentors, dedicated KIDS Foundation staff, and participants from all around Australia were delighted to catch up with old friends and welcome new survivors and volunteers into the support network. It is so important for those who have been physically altered by their injuries to have an opportunity to be free of stares and whispers for a few days. For new members in particular, to be among people who have been through similar experiences and to see how they have grown, developed, and taken control of their lives, is inspiring.

This experience is also often very confronting for newcomers, especially the volunteers. This is one reason we spend so much time at briefing sessions preparing participants and debriefing, to ensure they themselves do not experience post traumatic symptoms. It was the 20th Camp Phoenix and it was, once again, a year to remember. The children and their families enjoyed feeding dolphins, arts and crafts, tobogganing events, quad bike rides, and the PHOENIX "N" themed dress up party, which is usually a full-on disco, bit of Karaoke dancing night.

Every year since, Consolidated have made generous donations, ran events for KIDS, mentored children, attended camps as volunteers, and even arranged a working bee to clean and paint our new office at the Ballarat Airport. The Grant Family and the management team at Consolidated remain involved and hold a special place in the KIDS family today.

Our first KIDS Foundation Camp at Tangalooma in 2013 was an experience that, along with our team of Consolidated volunteers, we will never forget. On arrival, we were briefed by Susie and her staff and then paired off with survivors, siblings, parents, or grandparents. It was so heart-warming to witness the friendships that quickly developed in the days that followed. In a relaxed atmosphere, family members shared their stories with the volunteers, and the kids enjoyed the activities facilitated by the staff. We'll never forget Matt Thiele and his wonderful positive attitude. He is a standout role model for other survivors. We also appreciated the importance of the camp for siblings of survivors who so often have had to take a "back seat" as their parents needed to focus on the recovery of a brother or sister's injuries.

Following the camp, back at head office, we were so proud of our volunteers as they addressed the management team with moving accounts of their life-changing experiences. Since 2012, Consolidated has supported the KIDS Foundation, especially at its annual camps. The importance of sharing, recognising, and helping our people to grow is firmly entrenched in the Consolidated culture, so we are honoured to partner with Susie O'Neill and her team at the KIDS Foundation.

Coming together is a beginning.
Keeping together is progress.
Working together is success.

- HENRY FORD

Award Winning Partnership

You can't underestimate the lasting beneficial impact KIDS Foundation has on anyone it has contact with.

The KIDS Foundations prevention programs were growing in the Geelong region, and we were approaching companies for $5,000 sponsorships to run health and safety programs in local schools. One of the companies was Alcoa. Each company was paired with a school and had to complete a health and fitness challenge, which then funded a twelve-month safety program. Management from Alcoa were invited to engage with their partnered school and witnessed the program in action. That afternoon, I received a call to ask, "If the company donated $200,000 US dollars (which equated to about $260,000 AUS dollars at the time), what would you do with it?" Well, I had an answer on the spot. I was then asked to put it in writing, and they would take it to the next meeting. They did, and within a month, we received the news we were to be given the money, and it arrived soon after.

This donation became an annual part of our funding. We were proactive in providing constant feedback on the project, and individual staff members began volunteering at our camps and fundraising on our behalf. Alcoa invited us to accompany many activities and would often bring our young people that were survivors of burns to the Alcoa monthly barbeque and share some of the experiences we had at recent camps. About a year or so into the partnership, I was asked to come to a management meeting where they informed me that for some unknown reason the injuries at their site had decreased dramatically since they had partnered with KIDS. They decided that they would put a challenge to the workplace that for every injury free week that they had, we would receive $1,500. The following year we received an additional $78,000. This then led to two other sites joining the challenge and individuals from Alcoa personally fundraising. One year through the partnership, we received close to $500,000, made up of the annual donation, injury free days at three sites, a ball Alcoa held in Geelong on our behalf, and individual fundraising activities.

The Alcoa team became part of our extended family where we met some of the most beautiful, passionate people. An amazing couple, Brendan and Kylie, became embedded in our cause. They rode from Vietnam to Cambodia on a KIDS Foundation fundraiser where we became a "Sister Partner" to Hospital One in Vietnam - a bond that will stay with us forever. It hospitalises children with the most horrific burn injuries, most caused by street cooking. We delivered medical supplies, pressure garments, and gifts for their playroom. The sight of the children in the wards will be etched in our minds forever. Some of the crew on our trip were so traumatised by what they saw they had to leave the hospital and were given support following. The next year, we went back to renovate, painting the playroom and decking it out with new equipment, picture books, and toys, as well as giving financial donations individuals made. Kylie then joined our Board. One of the highlights of our partnership was jointly winning the Prime Minister's Awards for Excellence in Community Business Partnerships for Victoria.

As previously mentioned, I was often invited to some amazing functions that Alcoa held. Now my husband Brett isn't the sort of guy that loves attending formal functions. He is a tradie through and through. It is hard enough to get him to put on a suit for a wedding let alone to go to an event with a group of business-like people quite often wallowing in their egotistical self, so I would usually have a staff member accompany me. On this particular occasion, he would have wished he was there as he did enjoy reading crime stories. Matt Stevens, our General Manager at the time, and I went along and were separated onto two different tables. I remember jumping back into the car afterwards, both of us eager to share our stories, "You will never guess who was on my table."

After being ushered to a table, I sat down not knowing a soul and was introduced to each person. Sitting next to me was Andrew Fraser, who had attended with his partner, an employee at Alcoa. We started chatting, and when I asked what he did, he replied he was a criminal lawyer and author of crime based on time inside. I was later to find out Andrew Fraser was one of Australia's leading criminal lawyers, who defended underworld families like the Morans, the Pettingills, and businessman Alan Bond. With his success, he became a cocaine addict and ended up charged and sentenced in 2001 to seven years imprisonment with a minimum of five. He was sent to a maximum-security prison housing 38 of the most dangerous criminals in Victoria, one being serial killer Peter Dupas. Andrew Fraser had gone from a lawyer to a drug addict, a prisoner, and onto a best-selling author. I have since watched the TV series and documentaries on his life. As you could imagine, it was a very interesting dinner that night.

Our partnership with Alcoa continued for close to 10 years and ended when the Point Henry plant was basically shut down. All the beautiful people, some that stayed connected to the Foundation long after leaving Alcoa, like "Big Russ," will always be part of the KIDS family.

IF

Kylie Cirak and Brendan Foran share their experiences...

We were both working at Alcoa in community engagement and support roles when we first encountered the KIDS Foundation. As a large resources company, we were approached by so many worthy and wonderful community organisations doing excellent work, but there was something very special about KIDS Foundation. It wasn't just the crucial work they did assisting kids affected by injury and trauma, it was the spirit of the whole organisation and the commitment and energy of the staff and volunteers lead by their indefatigable founder, Susie O'Neill. Alcoa had a very strong focus on safety, so there was a natural values match. KIDS Foundation was determined to genuinely engage Alcoa staff, so it was more than just a sponsorship or typical corporate partnership - it was authentic partnership, both parties working to meet the needs and goals of the other. It was just a fabulous collaboration in so many ways.

As well as both professionally and at a personal level, we became involved in so many amazing initiatives. For us, the most memorable was our cycling trip through Vietnam and Cambodia to raise funds for KIDS Foundation. There was the physical challenge of cycling up to 100km a day in humid conditions, the emotional impacts of seeing the poverty experienced by so many Cambodians and learning about their torrid recent history, and the spiritual aspect of working as a team with people as committed to the cause as we were. It was life-changing in the best possible way.

The really unique aspect of this trip, and the impacts on us, was that the life-altering outcomes we experienced could be achieved through any KIDS Foundation activity. Attending a camp, meeting burn survivors, helping educate kids about safety, even cooking sausages to raise money. Any KIDS related event had the same magic quality. Working or volunteering, you felt that you were part of something real and amazing, that you were making a lasting contribution, that you were truly helping others, but that you were also helping yourself grow and improve as a person.

KIDS Foundation has an unwavering dedication to preventing injury and helping those who have been injured to recover. It does incredible work for those who have been injured and traumatised. But you can't underestimate the lasting beneficial impact it has on anyone it has contact with.

Through partnerships, we have been provided with opportunities to nurture innovative products and programs and create a real social impact through volunteering and employee engagement. I guess you could say our partnerships have been quite unique in structure and scope.

Cambodia 2005

The primary goal of our partnerships is to work with other organisations to reduce harm and injuries to children and provide support and care for those who have experienced traumatic circumstances.

The principles that structure our partnerships:

- Develop relationship of mutual trust, respect, and commitment.
- Agree upon values, goals, roles, processes, and measurable outcomes.
- Have clear, open, and accessible communication.
- Ensure feedback to, among, and from all stakeholders.
- Share the credit for accomplishments.
- Take time to develop and evolve.

Never underestimate the valuable and important difference you make in every life you touch.

- UNKNOWN

Rewriting The Future

NEWCASTLE PERMANENT CHARITABLE FOUNDATION

Another partnership that has played a pivotal role in the growth of the KIDS Foundation's prevention programs is Newcastle Permanent Charitable Foundation (NPCF). This is a partnership that has allowed KIDS Foundation to explore opportunities beyond monetary value, to scope and capture new resources of value, and to pilot innovation. Through NPCF, we have been provided with opportunities to nurture innovative products and programs and create a real social impact through volunteering and employee engagement. Each project that has started as a pilot has ended up as a national program. The most recent was based around a new book and supporting resources aimed at helping children understand their role in keeping themselves and others germ-free during the Coronavirus crisis. It was also designed to help children to recognise that they may be feeling a little anxious and provides ways to ease the uncertainty as well as teach them how they can help to prevent the spread of viral bugs. Due to the many non-speaking English families in regional NSW and Victoria, some families were not understanding the messages around the virus. NPCF provided us with additional funds to translate the book into four languages, Swahili, Arabic, simplified Chinese, and Vietnamese. Over a few months, approximately 60,000 copies of "SeeMore Bug Safety: The tiny germs we can't see" books were delivered to children in regional NSW, lock-down Melbourne, and through early childhood education centres Australia-wide free of charge.

The Charitable Foundation has the vision of rewriting the future for people in need, and Susie's work in shaping safe behaviours and making information accessible to all families provides a platform for young lives. Allowing them to flourish in safety and happiness aligns so well with this vision. Shared vision for change and impact is vitally important to the relationships with our partners, and there is no stronger example of this than our relationship with the KIDS Foundation. Susie's passion, evidenced-based programs, and an eye for engaging content for young people have enabled us to collaborate on seven projects over the past 12 years. In each case, we have been able to bring Susie's work to families in regional NSW who may otherwise not have access to the practical, fun learning programs delivered by the KIDS Foundation. The true test and demonstration of the power of this partnership has been shown when, in each case, the pilot collaboration between KIDS and the Charitable Foundation has led to government support to continue the program, extending and consolidating the program's impact.

A lasting relationship cannot exist without change, and we have proudly supported Susie as she has developed the KIDS Foundation's programs to build reach and relevance in a changing and increasing digital environments. Building on the early years of program rollout further into regional NSW, in 2018, we collaborated on a digitisation project that took SeeMore Safety online and into the classrooms and homes of tens of thousands more young children and their families. We then assisted as SeeMore Safety reached beyond the classroom and into the community, helping build connections and fostering conversation about safety between our youngest community members and our oldest, through the Connecting Generation Adopt a Grandbuddy program.

Most recently, Susie used her trusted position as a safety educator and advocate to develop a pandemic response program - SeeMore Bug Safety, which was the recipient of a Newcastle Permanent Charitable Foundation COVID Recovery grant. We also collaborated to bring the SeeMore Bug Safety book to four diverse language groups ensuring the important messages reach even more people, including those often overlooked.

We have proudly shared Susie's story of impact and development with our community and through our friends and families, and know how loved SeeMore Safety has become as a mascot for important messages of health and safety. We have also been lucky enough to share first-hand in the benefits that KIDS Foundation brings to our community. We have crossed the road safely with SeeMore, participated in fun classroom activities, and shared the joy of new intergenerational connections that Susie's work has empowered. Together, Susie, KIDS Foundation, and the Charitable Foundation have helped build healthy, safe, and resilient regional communities, which will have meaningful impact for generations to come.

The Newcastle Permanent Charitable Foundation has had a relationship with Susie and the KIDS Foundation since 2009.

For more than a decade, this partnership has worked to improve the lives of children in families in regional NSW through easily accessible, and fun to read, safety information.

by Graham NPCF

SEEMORE BUG
KIDS

Life's greatest rewards are reserved for those who help others succeed.

- SHANE PARRISH

She is our inspiration.

I had just returned from a four-day retreat with 105 young burn survivors and their carers. At our farewell dinner, we talked about people who inspired them the most. One of the young girls talked about Turia Pitt; she was her role model.

Turia, a beautiful ex-model and mining engineer, suffered life-threatening burns to 65% of her body and lost fingers after becoming trapped in a grassfire. At the time, she was competing in an ultramarathon through a remote area in the Kimberley region of Western Australia. She has since had more than 200 operations and defied expectations placed on her to chase down her wildest dreams. Turia has now competed in two Ironman Championships, one being the World Championships in Kona Hawaii, walked the Kokoda track, become a successful business entrepreneur, and authored three best-selling books. So, it isn't surprising to hear from our young people that she is their inspiration.

The kids at the camp suggested I try and get in touch with her and ask about becoming an ambassador for the Burn Survivors' Network. I had followed Turia's story for over two years and loved the way she communicated and connected with young people, so I sent an email. Her response read, "Yes, would be thrilled to be an ambassador for the Burns Survivors' Network, as well as be involved with the KIDS Foundation. What sort of events do you have coming up?"

We arranged to meet up the next time we were both in Sydney. There was a trip coming up, which involved taking some of our young survivors with me. The timing of the trip worked out perfectly because Turia could meet the children, talk to them directly, and share stories. We organised the meeting at one of our sponsor's, Verve Studio, office in Sydney. Being a photography studio, it allowed us to capture some fun images.

Turia had an ambition to compete in an Ironman, and as you would have read, Ironman was also my passion. Also, I really love it when KIDS can give back, and we were able to in this case. I asked Turia if she had a bike, which she didn't, so we arranged through Giant to organise a bike for her and Michael. I wondered how on earth she was going to operate the brakes with only a few fingers, but that was another one of the "defying the odds" challenges. KIDS was the Australian Ironman Championships Charity Partner at the time, and our fundraising activities were usually connected to it. Over the next few years, Turia was a guest speaker at some of our fundraising events and spoke at the Australian Ironman Championships Carbo night. A third of our income was connected to these events, so we were extremely grateful for the time Turia gave us.

I remember reading in Turia's book, UNMASKED, the section Michael writes where he talks about being overwhelmed with emotion as they leave the hospital knowing Turia will use all her strength to charge through her recovery, and that he "would be right by her side every step of the way." Friendships and relationships are so important in recovery. This by no means plays down Turia's strength and tenacity to live life every day to the fullest. But for some in recovery, the people they think would be there for them disappear. Although their loved ones may have good intentions, it's surprising how it turns out. It's too hard for them. For Turia, it was a very different story. She had a loving and devoted family, and the companionship and support Michael provided Turia throughout her whole journey was extra special, actually exceptional. Michael is one of those genuinely nice guys, as Turia put it, "Michael is definitively, and without a doubt, a pretty top bloke. He's kind, humble, generous, and loyal," and I guess within this book lives up to my values "Trust, Loyalty, and Kindness."

In 2016, Turia wrote wanting to let me know that she had really enjoyed being a part of the KIDS Foundation and had a lot of fun at the events that she had been involved with. But, unfortunately, she had to reduce her commitments. After a huge 2015, she could no longer commit to being an Ambassador. I really appreciated her honesty, as she had an affiliation with Interplast, and sometimes as an ambassador, it is best to devote time to one charity and do it well rather than a number and not have time to actually do anything. She was really lovely about it and wrote, "I hope you understand. Working with you and being a part of the KIDS Foundation has been a huge privilege, and this was not an easy decision to make. All the best, Turia."

K·I·D·S
Foundation
www.kidsfoundation.org.au
KIDS
FOUNDATION
CAMPS
Burn Survivors
NETWORK

We caught up for breakfast at the Australian Ironman Championships in Port Macquarie a few months later. We had both raced the day before. It was the first time Turia had competed at an Australian Ironman Championships, and she had an amazing race. We were chatting about the race, tying in our charity work, when Michael, who had joined us for breakfast, said something along the lines of, "Hey girls, I don't get that everything you achieve has to be all about the charity. It's okay to just do it for your own satisfaction." I had just been reminded of something that Brett had been telling me for years. He was spot on. I get so into the charity world that I forget that it is okay to do things for myself and not feel guilty for it. Turia did get to reach the pinnacle of Ironman when she was invited to compete in the Ironman World Championships in Kona, Hawaii in October that year. I followed the year after, and the night before the race, Turia sent a text message that gave me the inspiration I needed. The sort of inspiration our young people draw on in everyday life.

I'm a real fan of Turia's emails. I can't wait to see what comes next. Not only do I love the quirky way she writes, but there's also always something I can share with our young people to inspire them or something I can personally take from them. Would you believe, even how to win Monopoly? She says, "I'm competitive, a simple board game with me can get heated. Vicious. Brutal. And when I play with my family, who are all exceptionally similar when it comes to 'light-hearted games to pass the time'... things always get blown out of proportion," our family to a tee.

Late last year, Turia sent a box of her books The Good Selfie, which we gave to our teenagers for Christmas. They were thrilled. Ambassadors play such a crucial role in supporting our young people and in building KIDS Foundation's awareness and capabilities. Even when they are not able to continue in an Ambassador role, they usually remain connected in other ways and always hold a special place in our hearts.

I have taken on her nine
"hard-won experience" Monopoly tips:

1 Don't offer to be the banker.

2 Buy every property you land on.

3 Railroads aren't that great… but still buy them.

4 The orange properties are the best.

5 Buy as many houses as you can.

6 And on that note, don't buy hotels.

7 Put three houses on your property STAT.

8 DO buy yourself out of jail.
At the start of the game at least.
BUT as the game progresses, it's not a
terrible idea to stay in jail a little longer.

9. Be nice.

By Turia Pitt

Whoever changes one life,
changes the whole world.

- MICHELE AMITRANI, OMNILOGOS

DR. RICHARD HARRIS

"Real courage is what I see in ordinary people who face the same relentless challenges every day and still greet the dawn with a smile."

I was one of the many millions that followed the story that gripped the entire world in June 2018. Twelve boys and their coach from a Thai football team were trapped in the Tham Luang cave in Thailand. The worldwide rescue effort involved specialists and equipment from more than 17 countries. Among them were two experienced Australian cave divers, Dr. Richard Harris and Craig Challen, who were called into play a crucial role in rescuing them. Between July 8 -10, in stages, all twelve boys and their coach were rescued and survived.

On July 19, I sent a letter and a pack of information on the KIDS Foundation to Dr. Richard Harris's Anaesthetic Group in SA. I remember getting a call from "Harry" on August 6. It was memorable because I was in Tasmania in a noisy coffee shop waiting to go into a meeting regarding a grant when the call came through. I ran to find a quiet place and literally ended up in an open cupboard in the hallway. We had a chat about my request for Harry to become an Ambassador, and he agreed. I was so overwhelmed when he said he had received a lot of enquiries of a similar nature, but he chose us because of our principles around educating and empowering children to keep themselves safe, while still allowing them to be kids.

Harry's popularity grew even stronger after he and Craig were awarded the Star of Courage and Medal of the Order of Australia (OAM) by the Governor-General of Australia and in 2019 jointly awarded the Australian of the Year as a result of their involvement in the rescue. With Harry's new level of notoriety came numerous requests for guest speaking as he had made a name on the speaker's circuit for his inspirational storytelling and modesty. Harry rang to ask if he could donate his guest appearance speaking fees to us. Wow! That was like a dream come true, firstly giving his time to support us was honourable, but to raise funds for us was far beyond Harry's role as an Ambassador. Harry has attended numerous events for KIDS and even ran a unique fundraiser involving a small group guided dive of his very own underwater playground in SA.

Harry has been diving into the depths of these underground water-filled caves and gardens for over three decades, renowned worldwide as some of the greatest freshwater sinkholes in Australia.

Growing up in Adelaide life, was better than good. I think I realised I was lucky. Loving middle class parents, tightknit extended family, good schools, and good friends. Fortunate to the point of feeling guilty about it later in life. When life is like this, it is hard to imagine it as anything else. Young people don't think much about these things, but it would have been hard to put myself in the shoes of the kids from broken homes, those whose parents were doing it tough. It is something I think about more and more as I get older, and I think it pushes me to try and give something back.

Despite all those altruistic thoughts, the impetus for personal change didn't exactly come from within. I'll be honest and say that I might have continued on in my bubble if circumstances hadn't changed around me. Medical school, a full-time career, and a family of my own all swept me along on a path not too dissimilar to the way my life had begun; a life of comfort and safety that most of the world's population will never know. I worked hard but always made time for my passion of diving and exploration. Passions that were instilled in my childhood surrounded by small boats and the ocean.

Life certainly wasn't mundane. In my chosen medical field of anaesthesia, I sought out different experiences. Diving medicine, prehospital and retrieval medicine. Working overseas including the developing nation of Vanuatu. All these different spheres of work gave me an appreciation that even within my occupation, I wanted to challenge myself and stave off the boredom that can come with routine. And within my sport of diving, especially cave diving, I pursued the exploration and scientific opportunities with a vigour that gave me a strong sense of purpose and a zest for living. The act of controlled risk taking is immensely restorative and my personal way of recharging the batteries. And I was lucky to have chosen a field of endeavour that has a small number of disciples, and thus in which it is not too hard to establish a name for yourself.

Fast forward to 2018. I was sharing my work time between anaesthesia and the South Australian Ambulance Service in the retrieval section. For some years, I had been working to establish a cave diving rescue capability so that we could assist the emergency services in the event of a rescue or body recovery. And then in July 2018, 12 boys and their coach in a remote part of Thailand wandered into a complex cave system, only to become trapped behind fast rising monsoon floodwaters. Nine days later, they were found alive, cold, frightened, and starving, and I was contacted by the British divers who located them. Could I anaesthetise the boys to bring them out through 2.4km of flooded cave passages?

The rest as they say is history. My good friend Craig Challen and I assisted with the rescue, and we returned to learn that the news story had become a global one, and we appeared to be at the centre of it. A bravery award from the Australian government followed, a great deal of media interest, and finally we were awarded joint Australians of the Year for 2019. To be honest, we barely knew what had hit us. We felt intensely embarrassed by the attention, feeling that we had simply used our unusual skillset to help others in need. We were privileged to have the education to back us and the opportunity to be involved in a niche sport that we love. Who wouldn't assist the Thais in that situation?

What now? That was the thought on my mind as I sat on the couch flipping through some mail a few weeks after returning from Thailand. I had a strong sense that my life might have changed forever. I also had a sneaking feeling that it was time to step up and do something a little more worthwhile with this unexpected, slightly unwelcome, but nonetheless reality that was my new public "profile." So, I guess I was in a suggestive state of mind when one of the envelopes contained a letter along with some brochures from Susie O'Neill and the KIDS Foundation. Now you'll forgive me for thinking that Susie was the famous Olympic swimmer! In fact, both Susies are an integral part of the organisation; the CEO and Founder (who was writing to me) and the KIDS Ambassador (no relation!). But I remember thinking two things. Firstly, what an impressive cause; to help kids post trauma, burns, other injuries and to prevent this in the first place. And secondly, wouldn't it be cool to meet that swimmer!

Dr. Richard Harris (Harry) with Angelika, Belinda and Janine

The calls for me to become involved in various charities and organisations were mounting, so I made a conscious decision to choose just one or two and really do my best for them. I think my experience in Vanuatu treating injured kids in a very resource poor environment struck a chord. Let's face it, burns are awful and especially for young people who are building their identity and sense of worth. A disfiguring injury has a profound impact on their physical and mental wellbeing and can sentence them to a lifetime of medical interventions. And when I realised that many of these kids become injured through violence and abuse, well, it was easy to commit to doing my little bit.

My journey has been easy. Like travelling, sometimes you need to see how other people live to realise how good you have it at home. For me, the experience in Thailand has given me an extraordinary chance to pull my finger out and do something for others. I am sure the youth I have met through the KIDS Foundation have done more for me than I can do for them. I can only say I am honoured to be part of the Foundation working alongside some amazing people, and some even more inspirational youngsters.

Harry and Susie

As this book is about to go off to editor to be polished and refined, there is a movie about to be produced on Tham Luang cave rescue, and Harry's role is being played by Joel Edgerton. This is something like the email I sent to Harry on the morning of my own mini rescue.

Hey Joel Edgerton - aka Harry,

Congrats on the new movie role! Do you think the KIDS team could get a Guernsey to the opening night? Thought you might like this little mini rescue story! Doesn't quite cut the movie reel though!

I woke up at 4:30 a.m. this morning and made a pack with myself that today I would finish my book. I had just made some touching finishes to Giselle's story, the little girl who pulled a hot cup of tea over herself, when my sister and girlfriends rang to let me know they were heading for breakfast at the Vanilla cafe'. We were away for my sister Mandy's 60th birthday with a group of girls, on the last few days of a week of celebrations.

Sitting in the cafe', not long into breakfast, a baby let out an inconsolable, screaming cry, one of those helpless, could almost feel the pain, cries. A waitress had put down a hot boiling cup of tea on the table in reach of a 12-month baby girl. In a split second, she grabbed it and tipped it over herself. All hell broke out! My instinct was to get up and run after them toward the kitchen, then I heard the word "ice." Ice was coming out of the ice box about to land on her lap. NO! Not ice! Put her under cool running water. I insisted I knew what I was doing, and we found a trough and ran cool water over her. Her name was Matilda, the sweetest little thing, and listening to her cry was unbearable. She was screaming and fighting the pain. It was a wake-up call and reality check on the experiences the mums had described when they talk about burns in group sessions at camp. We must leave this cool running water over her for 20 minutes I insisted, although others were suggesting taking her out.

As luck had it, the pharmacist from down the road came running in and reassured them what we were doing the right thing. She needs to stay under cool running water for 20 minutes. I explained how this will prevent the sort of scarring that would have happened if we had done otherwise! Exactly around the 20 minutes, Matilda stopped crying and began playing in the water. Her little legs and tummy that were red raw, even purplish, had subsided considerably. She went off to hospital, and her mum sent a lovely message to say thank you and let us know that the doctors at the hospital were confident there will be no scarring. The staff member was extremely upset, and unaware of what to do in the case of a burn. She asked if I had anything they could put up for the staff to guide them what to do if a scald or burn incident was to happen again. By now, I had my educator and fundraising brain in action and onto an idea. My next book is SeeMore Safety and Hot Things - Hot water burns like fire!, which includes posters for cafés instructing how to serve hot drinks and food, what to do in a case like this, and activity sheets for children to keep them occupied.

Have a super great day movie star!
Kind regards,
X Susie

So, this ends the book. Hopefully if all you take from this book is what to do in the case of a hot water scald, then it has been all worthwhile. Nicky, a friend with me at the time, owns a restaurant and bar and sent a message to her 55 staff. We were both surprised that the staff and others really had no idea what to do.

Her message read...

Good morning everyone,

I've just been to a cafe' where a baby pulled a cup of tea on herself after a staff member placed it on the table in her reach. None of the staff knew what to do, so I thought I should share this with you:

1. Always place hot drinks and food out of reach of babies and young children.

2. Place the hot drinks on the table, don't hand them to the customer.

3. In the case of a burn, you must run cool water gently over the affected area for at least 20 minutes to reduce the heat and severity of the burn. This is hard if a child is crying, but the best action you can take.

4. Call an ambulance if needed. Regardless, it is best the parent takes them to have the burn check.

Can every single staff member acknowledge that you have read and understood this message?

Warm regards, Nicky

Burn Survivors
NETWORK
Living the dream under the
Limestone Coast!
Richard Harris
2019 Australian of the Year

No one who achieves success does so without acknowledging the help of others.

– ALFRED NORTH WHITEHEAD

Thanks

In the early 90's I attended a business workshop. On leaving we were asked to go to a book shop and purchase the first book that grabbed our attention. Sitting on the best seller stand was a book called "There's a lipstick in my briefcase: a guide for the new woman entrepreneur," by Cyndi Kaplan. I purchased it and read it on the plane on the way home. The book inspired me, so I decided to write to Cyndi, not expecting a reply, but she did. Long story short, on my next trip back to Sydney, Cyndi picked me up from the airport and we instantly connected. That was the start of a lasting and meaningful relationship, and I featured in her next book - "Awaken Your Business Creativity". Not only did Cyndi give me inspiration, but the knowledge I gained from that book has given me encouragement to write this book and to face difficult times with a "never-give-up attitude". Let's face it, there are plenty of those in charity life, especially financially. That is one reason why 28 years later this charity still exists, reaching more than 400,000 little people each year

As much as I love writing children's books, I never thought I would have the desire or time to write a book on my life. After completing my PhD in 2016, Professor Marilyn Fleer, my supervisor, and I were chatting, and she said that over the 10 years we worked together, she had seen me develop a passion for writing and I should use it to tell my story. Four years later, thanks to COVID, I had a little more time, one thing I was grateful for during the devastation this virus caused. The book started out to be written with Harry (Dr Richard Harris) about "Letting Kids Be Kids." Halfway into it, Harry said you have your own story to tell, so tell it. With advice from publishers and other authors, the book has been separated into two. The first, on my life and the KIDS Foundation, and soon to be published "Let Kids Be Kids" on raising happy, healthy, and safe children. Over 28 years, there have been some special individuals that have supported the creation of the KIDS Foundation. Family and friends have helped to raise funds during tough times, volunteered, attended numerous events, as well as given their love and guidance. There have been some pretty funny stories like the time my bestie, Tracey, had an unrelenting desire to star on TV. She was casted for one of our community service announcements and ended up in the Devondale cow suit.

Loving thanks to my special family for being so patient and tolerant, especially my husband, Brett, and our children, Matt, Emma, Ben, and Kate, who allowed my crazily active and imaginative mind to have some freedom to achieve what I have in my life. Along with Bella, this book is for them, their partners, Melita, Adam, Whittney, and Ricky, and our beautiful grandchildren, Bailey, Chase, Nellie, Lewi, Frankie, Bowie, Alfie, Bella, and the still to come little ones. Extra special thanks to Kate for being the sounding board for my thoughts, who with Teneille, shared my enthusiasm and encouraged and kept me motivated through the frustrating times. Teneille is a talented graphic designer that has been part of the Foundation for more than 16 years. Together we created the look and feel of the book. Also, to Dean Tonkin, who for many years has been the brilliant illustrator that has bought the characters and my work to life.

Thanks to the KIDS Board, Jo Stuckey (Chair), Matt Ricker, Rimas Liubinas, Margie Amarfio, Hamish McLachlan, Charles Kovess, Ian Coutts, and Athol Hodgetts, who share in the endeavours, ideas, and desires to make a difference to the lives of young children. Athol has been devoted to the Foundation for 28 years sharing the ups and downs of charity life. His sound best practice business advice has been integral in its survival.

My sincere gratitude to all the contributors to the book who gave their very valuable time to share their stories. A big thank you to the special children who have come into my life through the Foundation. You are inspirational and courageous and have given me purpose. Thanks to the hundreds of volunteers and KIDS Team, Janine Buesnel, Carlee Grant, Erynne Trotter, Nick Van Der Molen, Beau Jones, Teneille O'Connor, and Melissa Pearce, who have not only helped me realise the value of my work, but also continued the passion and furthered the commitment to reducing childhood harm and injury.

And finally, thank you for choosing this book and allowing me to share my life and the stories of these incredible people. Their stories are compelling, powerful and uplifting. I'm humbled by each person in this book and honoured to introduce them to you through "When bad things happen good things can grow".

Alone, we can do so little; together, we can do so much - HELEN KELLER Dr Carolyn Cogga
Dr Sally Cockburn Professor Marilyn Fleer Aaron Steel Aaron Freeland Abby Gilbert Ada
Alex Bialocki Alex Matthews Alison and Steve Hirth Alison and Christian McGee Alistair W
Andrea Chiasson Andrew Reid Andrew Sinclair Angie Lie Anita and Danny Frawley Ann an
Angie Lie Anita Hopkins Antony Bishop Athony Abbey Anthony Koutoufides Anthothy M
Champion Beau Jones Becky Lamb Belinda and Bertrum Birk Belinda Johnson Ben Gree
Brownless Blake Beck Brad and Annie Foster Brad McEwan Brad Spicer Brendan and Anc
Brad McEwan Bruce Snell Caleb Rixon Cam Coxford Carol Ann Land Carlee Grant Carlen
Colaciello Catherine Morrow Catherine Thiele Catherine Pitson Charles Kovess Chontelle
and Chantelle Doulis Chris Duett Chris Hannah Chris Kelly Chris Legh Chris and Tanya M
Handy Cipriano Corva Clint Kimmins Clinton Ball Cody Oliviera Colin Grime Con and Imr
Griffiths Cyndi Kaplan-Freiman Dallas O'Brien Daniel Terry Danny Cohen Damian Brown D
Dave Orlowski Dave Ross David Adams David Caple David Capper David Sinclair Daw
Denise Semple Delta Stinton Donald McKill Donna Carson Donna Gluyas Drew Ginn Edw
Emma Tuddenham Emma Wright Emma-Rose Parsons Eric Rosenberg Erika Orchard Erynn
Lawson-Smith Gary Peacock Gemma and Sue Bromley Geoff Meyer Geoff Hassan Georg
Gerrie Carr-MacFie Giselle Signorelli Glenda and John O'Neill Glenn Snell Grace Mc
Gwenda and Keith King Hamish McLachlan Hana Menzies Hannah Simmons Hayley Wi
Jacqui Frowen Jade Langley Jade Slater Jake Bridges Jamie and Andrea Mulcahy Jan M
McCartney Jennifer Hamilton-Browne Jennifer Jordan Jenny Carleton Jenny Lee Jess Flemn
Vallance Jodie Morris Josh Hilliard John Davis John and Mary Grant John Minto John Mes
Grant Justin Lacko Kaisey Gordon Kane Bowden Kane McErvale Karen Jacques Karla Bak
Kate Major Kate Narev Katie Sewell Katherine Kelly Katherine Wirth Kathryn Quinlan Kati
Cook Kendal and Steve Harrison Kerry Britt Kerrie Kluss Kevin Sheedy Kim and Paul Courtn
Mann Laurie Cook Lee Troop Leeann Lloyd Leanne McPherson Leanne Smith Leanne South
Lin Eng Lindsay Carey Lisette and Mark Seery Lockie Clancy Lou Panaccio Luc Evans Luke
Neil Trevena Mandy and Steve Troon Marcus Altmann Margie Amarfio Mark Guinea Mark
Martin Ryan Martine Jager Marty Sharpels Mary and John Grant Mary White Matt Brack
Welsh Maureen Lynch Max Walker Maxine Trembath Megan Ballantyne Megan Urlichs
Michael Hands Michael Huxley Michael Gilmour Michael and Marita Lysaght Michael R
Darren Postlethwaite Mick Fettes Mick Frazer Mike Rabbitt Mike Riley Murray Sallaway N
Peresso Nick Clare Nick Croft Nick Gilbert Nick Green Nick Kane Nicky and Danny Quinl
Bann-Murray Paul Beseler Paul Dawson Paul Grant Paul Harragon Pauline Molloy Penny
Sarah Bradford Philip Archer Professor Hedley Peach Rachel Bell Renee Ball Renee Chakao
Rob Taylor Robbie and Rose Hunter Robert Osmotherly Robyn Thinn Rod Barnaby Rod Vine
Sarah Kearney Sarah Lia Sasha Hurrell Scott Dowsett Scott McPherson Scott Morrison PM
Sofi and Damian McKeegan Sophie and Sam McGuane Sam Smith Shayne and Steven
Coombs Steve Gilbert Steve Menhenett Steve Moneghetti Steven Southwell Stuart Fox Sus
Spratling Tammy Smith Tanya Lawless Therese Nichols Tiffany Callaghan Tiffany Loftus H
Tracey and Tom Frawley Tom Moore Tony Frawley Trent Taylor Trevor Meade Trevor Webb

Dr Joanna McMillan Dr Laurie Prosser Dr Lindsay Carey Dr Richard Harris Dr Rimas Liubinas
and Jacqui Boas Adrian Calleri Adriel Young Alan Cransberg Alan Freedman Alex Smith
x (Andino) Andrew Hall Andrew Wellington Angela Nicolades Angelika and Brian Hannon
Anna Barlow Anna Fry Annie and Anna Louey Annie Davis Anna Sullivan Anne Whitehead
and Chris Eade Amy Gillet Ari Suss Athol and Lola Hodgetts Bailey Tuddenham Barbara
Beth Bromley and Phil Sherry Berrick Wilson Bev and John Creagh Bevan Addinsall Billy
an Foran Brett O'Neill Brett and Di Tynan Brett Hilker Brittney Tasker - Gilbert Brodie Young
os Melegrito Carol McDougall Caroline Smyth-Roberts Caroline Yates Casey Barnes Cathy
Hilliard Chris Powell Cliff Farley Craig Jansen Craig Willian Chris Ball Chris Browne Chris
t Christian Schwaezler Christine Wellington Christie and Dane Johnston Ciaran and Karon
aig and Neri Alexander Craig Buesnel Craig Jansen Craig Strudwick Craig Willian Crystal
n Darren Fox Darren McClenaghan Darren and Sophie Rutherford Darren Rix Dave O'Neill
onkin Debbie and Simon Gilbert Debbie Lewis Decheng Ma Dee Howes Denise Drysdale
e Hehir Eliza Hoppe Elizabeth Ebli Emma Cleary Emma Conn Emma O'Neill Emma Phillips
Coulthard Fad**dy Zo**uki Fran S**ignore**lli Frank D**onnelly** Gail Rodgers **Gary Hump**hreys Gary
Varelas Geor**gene** Bridgema**n Geo**rgie Mo**rrison G**eoff and Id**a Schw**ind **Gerard** Donnelly
Orr Graham B**atten** Graham **and Tr**acey **Bradfor**d Greg Presto**n Gr**eg Stewa**rt Guy** Leech
Val Brew Heat**her C**leland Hel**en Alle**n **Helen B**urge Holly McE**rvale I**an Coutts Ian Masson
iller Janet an**d Pete**r Jones Ja**nine** B**uesnel J**ake Bridges Jason **Bourke Jason** and Nerissa
glas **Jill an**d John **B**urt Jim Cai**l Jo Hall Jo King** Jo Stuckey Joanne Yo**ussef Jodi Ditte**rich Jodi
John **Osbo**rne **Joh**n Schreen**an Julian** Fie**ld Julia**nne Adams Julie Bond Julie **Schmoc**k Justin
ran Han**dy Karen W**atson Kat**alin Bl**ond Kat**e Hillia**rd Kate Fau**lman**n Kate Betts **Kate H**assell
g Katie Se**well Katri**na Ashton **Kay** Vargas Ke**ith Glo**ver Keith K**ing Ke**l Kerr Kel**lie Du**nn Ken
ylie and Ge**off Bake**r Kylie Cir**ak Ky**lie Maher **Lachlan** Piggot Lau**ra Lunty Lauren Dic**k Lauren
Leonie Miller **Liam K**ennedy Lib**by M**cLean Lisa C**olema**n Lisa Edwa**rds Lisa and P**eter Thiele
er Luke Young Lydia Martin Lydia McGuigan Lydia Whiteside Lynda Simmons Mandee and
il Marnie McPherson Marg and Brian Gallagher Marlene and John Rodgers Martin Clucas
Matthew Ricker Matt Golinski Matt Kirwin – Hamilton Matt and Jo Stevens Matt Thiele Matt
Melanie Water Melinda Meade Melissa Pearce Marianne Collopy Michael Bridgeman
Thorpe Michelle Ferris Michelle Harris Michelle McMahon Michelle O'Brien Michelle and
Nathan Tracey Neil Taylor Nella Santisi Nicholas Van Der Molen Nicholas Waring Nicole
Nicole Fraser Nicole Peresso Nigel Durbridge Oliver Scott Oscar Mulcahy Paul Adler Paul
d David Woods Pete Murray Pete O'Neill Peter Thompson Peter Viska Phil Duggan Phil and
nce Rhys Perrin Rhyss Oxenford Richard Lyle Ricky Jeffs Ricky Tasker - Gilbert Rob McDonald
Rossanna Faraci Russell Watson Ryan Pinnick Sally Skelton Sally Tebble Samuel Blackadder
Shane Snibson Shane Smith Shane and Kelly Viney Shannon Simone Segrave Sigrid Wallis
chultz Sheree and Mark Gilbert Stephanie Field Stephen Hewett Stephen McIntyre Steven
Hammond Susan Pollard Sue and Mark Hancock Sue Foley Sue Harry Susie O'Neill Susie
Tina Benoit Teneille O'Connor Teressa Tommy McIntosh Tony and Sue Barber Tony Dekker
Pitt Varli Blake Vanessa Moule and Scott Diete Voula Mallios Wayne Linekar Zoi Penoglou

My Wish

My wish is that every child is safe - free from harm and injury.

Through the KIDS Foundation I'm committed to keeping little people safe by educating and empowering them and the whole community in harm and injury prevention. We value the contributions children make and encourage agency in their own learning, in a creative safe space. KIDS Foundation celebrates little people from all family cultures, faiths, genders, and sexualities. For all the millions of children who have been harmed and injured, and cannot speak for themselves, one day will have a voice and will be able to share it. Every child has the right to be safe, free from harm and injury, and it's everybody's responsibilities to ensure this happens.

There some messages that I would like to encourage others to think about:

Don't be quick to judge, because everyone has a story.

Others stare because they are curious, so make their stares worthwhile and give them a smile.

There is always a way to do things that seem impossible. You just have to want to find it.

Everybody can use a little bit of kindness in their life and you can be the one to provide it.

Trust is built and earned over time. It involves courage and taking a risk. When someone has your trust it is a compliment and is integral to a happy relationship.

And, remember when bad things happen, good things can grow.

Professional images that appear throughout the book have been kindly provided by Verve Portraits and Carol's photos by Photographer Brian Cassey.

CPSIA information can be obtained
at www.ICGtesting.com
Printed in the USA
LVHW082258190721
693164LV00007B/334/J